TIME FOR KIDS READERS

Teacher's Guide
Grade 4

Harcourt

Orlando   Austin   Chicago   New York   Toronto   London   San Diego

Visit *The Learning Site!*
www.harcourtschool.com

TIME FOR KIDS READERS

Table of Contents

© Harcourt

Life in a Canyon

BACKGROUND

Summary

The Grand Canyon is a spectacular landform that draws many tourists each year. Havasu Canyon is a smaller canyon nearby. Although no roads go there, a group of Native Americans calls Havasu Canyon home. The Havasupai have lived in the canyon for hundreds of years, and many still do.

READING TIPS

Building Background

■ Encourage students to share what they know about the Grand Canyon. Elicit words that describe the canyon. (Possible responses: rocky, hilly)

FAST FACTS

■ The Grand Canyon lies in northwestern Arizona.

■ The Grand Canyon is 227 miles (365.3 km) long and as much as 18 miles (29.0 km) wide. It is nearly 1 mile (1.6 km) deep.

■ Europeans first discovered the canyon in 1540, when a group of Spanish explorers led by Francisco Vásquez de Coronado encountered it on an expedition from Mexico (which was called New Spain at the time).

■ When the Spanish first arrived, Native Americans had already been living in the canyon for several hundred years.

■ In the mid-1800s, the United States Army began to explore the canyon more fully. It was during this period that the United States government set up a reservation for the Havasupai.

■ Ask students if they know how a canyon is formed. (Moving water, such as a river or stream, wears away rock bit by bit, creating a canyon over the course of millions of years.) To jumpstart ideas, point out that the Colorado River flows through the heart of the Grand Canyon.

Reading for Details

■ How did the Colorado River form the Grand Canyon? (The flowing water of the river slowly wore away the land and rocks.)

■ What does the name Havasupai mean? (the people of the blue-green water)

■ What is the name of the village in which the Havasupai live? (Supai)

■ What is an easy way to get to Supai? (on horseback)

■ How many people live in Supai? (about 450)

■ What is the name for the land that the government gives Native Americans to live on? (a reservation)

■ Why do people visit Havasu Canyon and Supai? (to camp in the canyon, to swim in the creek, to admire the falls)

■ Why did the Havasupai begin to accept visitors? (Tourism brought in money and created jobs.)

Critical Thinking

■ Discuss why Native American people might have decided to settle in a canyon hundreds of years ago. How might the canyon's setting and resources have been useful to them? (Overhanging rocks would have provided shelter from sun and rain; the river at the bottom of the canyon would have provided water for drinking and washing.)

■ Ask students if they would like to live in a place that was accessible only on foot, by horse, or by helicopter. What advantages would there be in living in such a place? (Possible responses: a peaceful atmosphere, privacy, access to natural resources) What disadvantages might there be? (Possible responses: less contact with people from outside the canyon, fewer modern conveniences)

Activity

■ **Where Is It?:** Have students locate the Grand Canyon and the Colorado River on a classroom map. If possible, reproduce maps of Arizona and challenge students to find Havasu Canyon, Havasu Creek, and the village of Supai. If the map includes details, notice the absence of roads leading to Supai.

Vocabulary

Havasu Canyon: a small side canyon off the Grand Canyon in Arizona

Havasupai: Native American people who live in Havasu Canyon

Supai: the village in which the Havasupai live

EXTENSION ACTIVITIES

CREATE-A-CANYON

Curriculum Areas: Social Studies/Geography, Science
Skills: Understanding Natural Formations, Cause and Effect, Experimentation, Group Work

Encourage students to explore how a river forms a canyon. Divide the class into groups of three or four students each. Give each group a plastic tub, a bag of sand or gardening soil, and a watering can with a narrow spout. (A measuring cup or an empty milk jug will also work.) Instruct students to fill the tub about halfway with the sand or soil, making the top of the soil as smooth as possible. Then have students fill the can with water and take turns pouring the water in a straight line, back and forth, across the top of the soil or sand. Students will observe that the continuous flow of water forms a trough in the soil, creating a small "canyon" in their plastic tubs. Ask: What does this experiment reveal about the formation of the Grand Canyon and Havasupai Canyon?

STARTING A BUSINESS

Curriculum Area: Social Studies
Skills: Understanding Points of View, Oral Language, Reasoning

Divide the class into groups of four students each. Each group will role-play a skit that involves four characters: two Havasupai people from Supai and two tourists who would like to set up a business there. Have each group brainstorm a list of the types of businesses that outsiders might like to start in

Supai. A pair of artists might like to set up an art gallery, for instance, while a pair of entrepreneurs might want to operate a popular food chain restaurant or a movie theater. Ask students to consider the ways that such a business might improve the town of Supai, as well as the ways it might interfere with the Havasupai way of life. After each presentation, challenge students to decide if the proposed business would be good for Supai. Why or why not?

COME AND VISIT!

Curriculum Area: Language Arts
Skills: Descriptive and Persuasive Writing

Distribute copies of page 4. Explain to students that their job is to create a travel brochure, enticing tourists to visit Havasu Canyon and Supai. Discuss the headings for each brochure panel. Tell students to write their brochure copy on the lines and to illustrate their copy in the blank spaces of each column. Display the completed brochures on a bulletin board for students to view and discuss.

ANSWER KEY

COPYING MASTERS

Page 3 1. B, **2.** F, **3.** C, **4.** E, **5.** A, **6.** G, **7.** D

Page 4 Students should include at least two details about Havasu Canyon or Supai under each heading. Illustrations should clearly correspond to the text.

READER

Think and Respond 1. Supai mail deliveries include letters, food, business and school supplies, medicines, and computers. **2.** Over millions of years, slow-moving streams wear away rock bit by bit, eventually forming a canyon. **3.** Modern-day Supai life is quiet. People shop, plant crops, and host tourists; children go to school and play. **4.** Canyons are scenic and a good place to observe nature; however, canyons are prone to severe flooding and getting supplies to the area can be difficult. **5.** Students should support their opinions with evidence from the Reader.

Do Research Students' presentations should include accurate geographical details. Encourage students to use visuals to support their research.

Name_____

Havasupai History

The events below tell about the Havasupai, but they are out of order. Put the events in the correct time sequence and rewrite them in the column to the right.

A. After nearly 100 years, the United States government gives the Havasupai much more land to live on.

1. _____

B. Havasupai people live in the canyon.

2. _____

C. The United States Army begins to explore.

3. _____

D. Today, Supai has a motel, a café, and a store.

4. _____

E. The United States government restricts the Havasupai to a small reservation.

5. _____

F. Spanish explorers arrive in the 1500s.

6. _____

G. Tourists begin to visit Supai and Havasu Canyon.

7. _____

Now use these notes to write a short report about the history of the Havasupai people. Refer to *Life in a Canyon* for more details about each event.

_____

_____

_____

_____

_____

_____

_____

_____

_____

Come and Visit!

Invite tourists to visit Havasu Canyon and Supai. Write about the area in the brochure outline. Follow the headings. Draw pictures to illustrate your brochure, too.

Getting There

Things to See and Do

History

TIME FOR KIDS READERS
Walks in the Wilderness

BACKGROUND

Summary

Two children set off with their families to hike two different nature trails. Amanda is hiking the Appalachian Trail in the East, while Brandon is hiking the Pacific Crest Trail in the West. Through e-mail messages, the hikers compare their adventures and experiences along these scenic trailways.

READING TIPS

Building Background

■ Draw a two-column chart on the chalkboard. Title one column "West Coast" and the other column "East Coast." Invite students to imagine the wilderness of each area. How might the wilderness of the eastern United States differ from that of the western United States? List students' ideas in the appropriate columns of the chart.

■ Have any of the students ever been hiking? If so, invite them to share their experiences and impressions. If not, ask them to imagine what they might see or do on a hike.

Reading for Details

■ What do *AT* and *PCT* stand for? (*AT* stands for "Appalachian Trail." *PCT* stands for "Pacific Crest Trail.")

■ How are Amanda and Brandon able to communicate? (via e-mail, when their families are able to hook up to a telephone line)

■ On which day does Amanda start hiking the Appalachian Trail? (Friday, June 1)

■ On which day does Brandon start hiking the Pacific Crest Trail? (Saturday, June 2)

■ Why don't Brandon and his family begin hiking at the very start of the Pacific Crest Trail? (It is too hot in the summer to hike the southern portion of the trail through the desert.)

■ Why does Amanda sign her letter "Too Fast"? (because her parents tell her she is walking "too fast")

■ Why does Brandon sign his letter "Boots"? (because his father says his feet are so big that he is all "boots")

■ Which mountain is the highest in the lower 48 states? Which trail is it on? (Mt. Whitney; the Pacific Crest Trail)

■ Which tall building can Amanda see from the Appalachian Trail? Where is she when she sees this building? (the Empire State Building; Bear Mountain)

Critical Thinking

■ Ask students if they think designated nature trails are a good idea. What purpose do these designated trails serve? (Possible responses: By limiting human traffic to certain areas, designated trails help preserve

FAST FACTS

■ The Pacific Crest Trail is 2,650 miles (4,264 km) long and runs through three states—California, Oregon, and Washington.

■ The Appalachian Trail is 2,167 (3,487 km) miles long and runs through 14 states—Georgia, Tennessee, North Carolina, Virginia, Maryland, West Virginia, Pennsylvania, New Jersey, New York, Connecticut, Massachusetts, Vermont, New Hampshire, and Maine.

■ The Pacific Crest Trail begins at the border of Mexico and ends at the border of Canada.

■ The Pacific Crest Trail passes through these national parks: Sequoia/Kings Canyon National Parks, Yosemite National Park, Lassen Volcanic National Park, Crater Lake National Park, and the North Cascades National Park complex.

■ The Appalachian Trail is in the Appalachian Mountains and passes through Great Smoky Mountains National Park and Shenandoah National Park.

other areas; designated trails prevent people from getting lost in the woods.)

■ Ask students where they would prefer to hike— on the Appalachian Trail or on the Pacific Crest Trail—and why.

Activity

■ **Getting Ready:** Invite students to consider what they would bring with them if they went hiking for several months along a scenic nature trail. To enhance the activity, you might bring to class an empty backpack and possible hiking items, such as various types of food, a flashlight, a large radio, a waterproof poncho, and so on. Have students place items in the backpack and then test the backpack's weight. Ask students to consider which items are necessary and which ones might be left behind if the pack is too heavy.

Vocabulary

altitude sickness: a physical condition someone can get when he or she is too high above sea level

caretaker: a person whose job is to look after a building, property, or other people

hiker: a person who takes long walks, especially in the country

pass: a low place between mountains

trek: to make a slow, sometimes difficult, journey

wilderness: an area of wild land where no people live, such as a dense forest

EXTENSION ACTIVITIES

HIKING DOS AND DON'TS

Curriculum Areas: Social Studies/Ecology, Art, Language Arts
Skills: Environmental Awareness, Making Inferences, Drawing
    Conclusions, Graphic Design, Oral Presentation

Briefly discuss with students the things one should and should not do when hiking or camping on a nature trail. For example, is leaving garbage behind a good idea? Is it wise to leave out food that might attract bears? Tell students to read through the story and to make a list of dos and don'ts that are essential for maintaining a wilderness environment while keeping hikers and campers safe. Ask students to create information posters that could be posted

along a hiking trail. Invite students to share their posters and explain to classmates their chosen dos and don'ts.

SUPER KID HIKERS OF THE WORLD

Curriculum Area: Language Arts
Skills: Exchanging Ideas, Interviewing, Creative Thinking,
    Improvisation

At the end of the book Amanda calls herself "super kid hiker of the world." Suppose that a newspaper reporter was also impressed that Amanda and Brandon hiked such large portions of the Appalachian and Pacific Crest Trails. Ask students to come up with a list of questions to ask either Amanda or Brandon about their experiences. Divide the class into groups and have each group role-play a skit that includes Amanda, Brandon, and a few reporters. As the reporters ask questions, encourage the students playing Amanda or Brandon to answer freely, recalling information from the book.

ANSWER KEY

COPYING MASTERS

Page 7 Students' postcard messages and illustrations should reflect specific information from the Reader.

Page 8 Students should include at least two specific details from the Reader in each section of the chart.

READER

Think and Respond 1. Hikers carry a small water filter that looks like a pump. **2.** People enjoy being one with nature, experiencing physical challenges, or seeing beautiful scenery. **3.** The trails are so long that hikers will pass through five climate zones, each with its own weather patterns and temperatures. **4.** Students' name choices should reflect their personal characteristics or backgrounds.

Keep a Journal Students' journal entries should be chronological and should include specific details about weather and other environmental features.

Postcard Messages

Create a postcard from either Brandon to Amanda or Amanda to Brandon, describing a special day on the trail. Write the message on the lines. Draw a postcard picture in the box.

AT vs. PCT

Amanda and Brandon saw different sights as they hiked along the Appalachian and Pacific Crest Trails. Compare the things they saw by filling in the chart.

	Amanda (AT)	Brandon (PCT)
Animals		
Plants		
Landforms		
Historic Sites		
States		

© Harcourt

Earthquake!

BACKGROUND

Summary

Earthquakes can be as surprising as they can be deadly—as the people of New Madrid, Missouri, learned all too well when an unexpected series of earthquakes destroyed their town in 1811–1812. In the years since then, scientists have tried to unravel the mysteries surrounding earthquakes and their causes.

READING TIPS

Building Background

■ Invite students to share what they know about earthquakes. You might write the word on the board and then draw a vertical line separating the individual words *earth* and *quake*. Challenge students to define each part of the word and then to explain the entire word's meaning.

FAST FACTS

■ Scientists believe that small earthquakes occur on the planet about once every thirty seconds.

■ Many earthquakes occur along the edge of the Pacific Ocean. Scientists call this the Pacific Ring of Fire. California, Mexico, and Alaska are along this ring.

■ Just as the continents have names, so do the plates of the earth's crust. The United States is on the North American plate.

■ The San Andreas Fault is the line between the North American plate and the Pacific plate.

■ A seismograph is an instrument that detects earthquakes and measures their power. Scientists who study seismographs are called seismologists.

Reading for Details

■ How long ago did the earthquakes in New Madrid, Missouri, occur? (about 190 years ago, in 1811–1812)

■ On which layer of the earth do people stand? (the crust)

■ What does an earthquake monitoring station do? (It keeps track of all earthquakes, even the small ones.)

■ What do geologists do? (They study the history of the earth and how it was formed.)

■ What is the significance of the Reelfoot Rift? (It is the cracked rock that caused the earthquakes in New Madrid, Missouri.)

■ Which earthquakes are usually more powerful— the earthquakes west of the Rocky Mountains or east of the Rocky Mountains? (those east of the mountains)

■ How do most people get hurt during an earthquake? (by falling buildings and debris)

■ How would a rubber foundation prevent a building from collapsing during an earthquake? (by preventing the building from shaking too much)

Critical Thinking

■ After students read the book, challenge them to describe the process that leads to an earthquake. (Tectonic plates float on the mantle beneath the earth's crust, often sliding over or rubbing up against each other. Sometimes two plates get stuck against each other. Pressure between the two plates builds up over the course of many years. When the pressure becomes too much, the plates move with tremendous force, causing seismic waves to travel through the earth's crust, shaking the ground and everything on it.)

Activity

■ **Deskquakes:** Push together several student desks and ask students to imagine that each desk is a tectonic plate. Have students cover the desk surfaces with paper, books, pencils, and other objects to represent buildings and other structures on the earth's surface. Then ask a student to help you push one desk along another so the edges rub. Have students observe and describe what happens to the items on the desks. Check students' understanding by asking them to describe how the movement of tectonic plates causes items on the earth's surface to shift and shake.

Vocabulary

crust: the hard, outer layer of the earth

epicenter: the area directly above the place where an earthquake occurs

fault: a large crack in the earth's surface that can cause an earthquake

geologist: a person who studies the earth's layers of soil and rock

mantle: the part of the earth between the crust and the core

seismograph: an instrument that detects earthquakes and measures their power

tectonics: the geology of structural changes in the earth's crust

EXTENSION ACTIVITIES

SEISMIC GRAPHS

Curriculum Areas: Science, Math
Skills: Interpreting and Recording Data, Graphing, Research

Distribute copies of page 11. Review the purpose of a bar graph (to compare related information). Then instruct students to create a bar graph showing the magnitude of various earthquakes on the Richter scale. Have students refer to their graphs as they answer the questions at the bottom of the page.

REPORTERS ON THE SCENE

Curriculum Area: Language Arts
Skills: Creative Thinking, Descriptive Writing, Inferring, Oral Language

A big earthquake is big news. Ask students to imagine that a major earthquake has hit their area and that they are reporters on the scene, informing people around the country about what is happening in their community. Have students write television news reports about the imaginary quake. Tell students to consider the specific impact an earthquake might

have on their particular community as they write their reports. Which buildings, businesses, or natural features might suffer the worst effects? If possible, have students videotape their reports and then play them for the rest of the class.

ANSWER KEY

COPYING MASTERS

Page 11 Students' graphs should reflect the data.

Page 12 1. New Madrid, **2.** plates, **3.** epicenter, **4.** seismograph, **5.** Richter scale, **6.** geologist, **7.** mantle; **Final Phrase:** The World Series

READER

Think and Respond 1. Alaska; **2.** because the fault is so long and runs through well-known cities such as Los Angeles, Hollywood, and San Francisco; **3.** the Richter scale; It measures the ground motion an earthquake causes on a scale from 1 to 8; **4.** The mantle is the hot layer of thick liquid rock on which the earth's crust floats. Tectonic plates are giant pieces of the earth's crust, sometimes thousands of miles across. The cracks between the plates are called faults; when pressure builds between the faults, the plates move with tremendous force, causing an earthquake. **5.** Dos: If indoors, duck under a desk or table; keep away from windows, fireplaces, and large appliances; if outdoors, stay away from buildings, power lines, and tall poles; if in a car, stay there. Don'ts: Don't use stairs while a building is shaking; don't turn on stove or use matches; don't use the phone unless it's an emergency.

Do Research Students' diagrams or models should be labeled accurately.

Name_____

"Seis-ing" It Up

Create a bar graph in the space below. Color in each bar to show the strength of the earthquake according to the Richter scale.

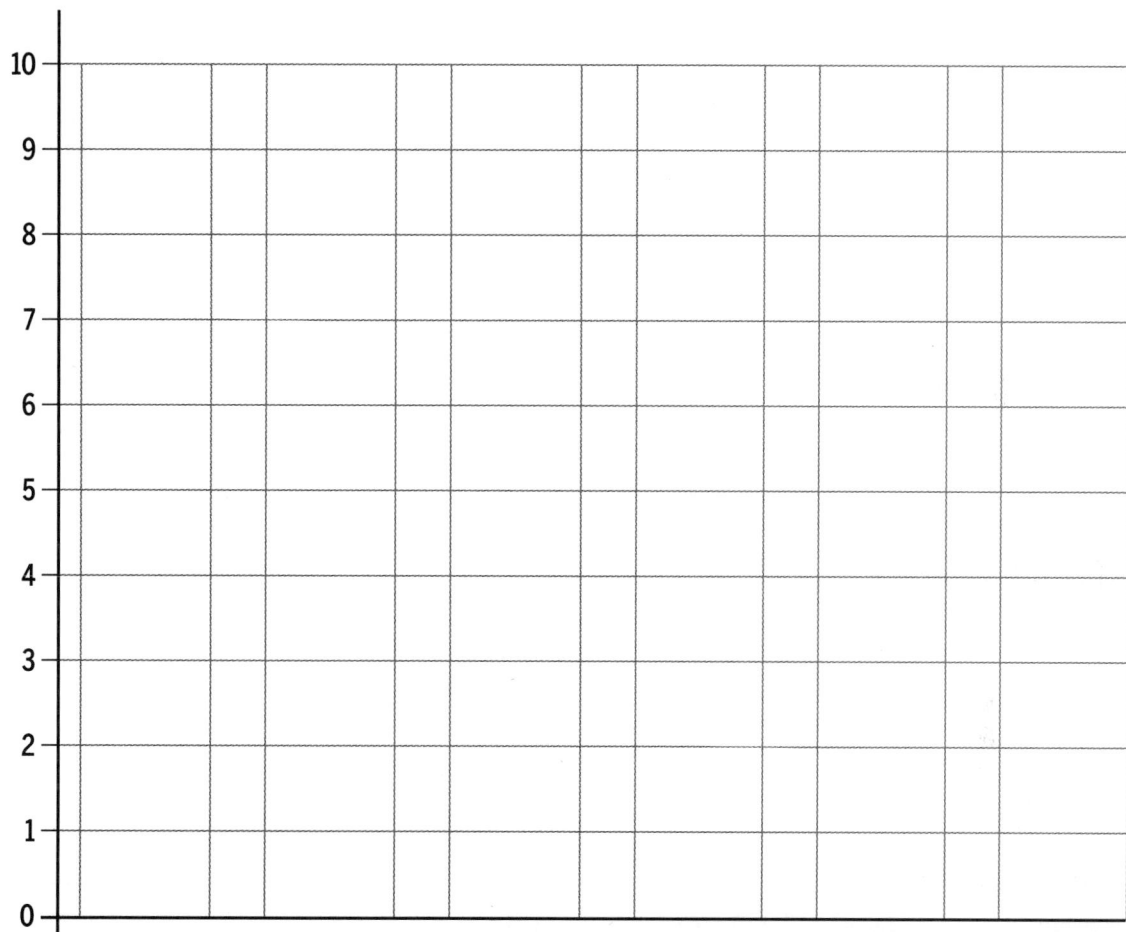

10					
9					
8					
7					
6					
5					
4					
3					
2					
1					
0					

| 1906 San Francisco, California **8.3** | 1920 China **8.6** | 1960 Chile **9.5** | 1964 Prince William Sound, Alaska **9.2** | 1985 Mexico **8.1** | 1988 Armenia **6.9** |

Bonus: What was the date and place of the strongest earthquake? Use an encyclopedia, research books, or the Internet to find out more about the earthquake and the damage it caused. Then use an atlas to find the earthquake's exact location.

Sports Cut Short

In October 1989, an earthquake rocked San Francisco. Which sporting event was taking place when the earthquake struck? Complete the sentences to find out. Write the answers on the lines. Then write the numbered letters in the spaces at the bottom of the page. The words in the box will help you.

Word box:
- epicenter
- geologist
- mantle
- New Madrid
- plates
- seismograph
- Richter scale

1. In 1811 and 1812, earthquakes destroyed the town of
___ ___ ___   ___ ___ ___ ___ ___ ___ , Missouri.
        4   8

2. Large pieces of the earth's crust that move are called tectonic
___ ___ ___ ___ ___ ___.
    7   13

3. The area directly above where an earthquake happens is the
___ ___ ___ ___ ___ ___ ___ ___ ___.
            10   6

4. A machine that helps track earthquakes is a
___ ___ ___ ___ ___ ___ ___ ___ ___ ___ ___.
9   5

5. A system for rating the strength of an earthquake is the
___ ___ ___ ___ ___ ___   ___ ___ ___ ___.
11   2

6. Someone who studies the earth's rocks and soil is a
___ ___ ___ ___ ___ ___ ___ ___ ___.
                12 14

7. The layer of earth beneath the crust is the
___ ___ ___ ___ ___ ___.
        1   3

The sporting event that was interrupted because of an earthquake was
___ ___ ___   ___ ___ ___ ___ ___   ___ ___ ___ ___ ___ ___.
 1   2   3   4   5   6   7   8   9   10 11 12 13 14

EARTHQUAKE!

A Fisher's Life

BACKGROUND

Summary

For thousands of years, people have fished the world's oceans. Native Americans of the northeastern United States caught a variety of fish, the most plentiful of which was cod. When European settlers first arrived, they also took advantage of the immense quantities of fish available. Over the centuries, however, fish populations have grown smaller, a fact that many people attribute to overfishing.

READING TIPS

Building Background

■ Have students consider how fish arrives on people's tables. Where does the fish come from? Who catches it? How is it caught? List students' ideas on a piece of chart paper to check after reading.

■ Talk with students about what life on the seas might be like for professional fishers. What challenges might professional fishers face? (Possible responses: dangerous weather conditions, a dwindling supply of fish, economic problems)

Reading for Details

■ Which ocean, and which aspect of ocean life, is this book about? (fishing in the North Atlantic)

■ What is significant about West Passamaquoddy Head, Maine? (This is the first place in the United States over which the sun rises .)

■ Why is it important that the Gulf Stream current brings plankton with it? (Plankton is food for many fish, such as cod, which is why North Atlantic waters usually have an abundance of fish.)

■ Which people were the first to fish off the coast of northern North America? (Native American people)

■ Why did things change for the Native Americans in the 1500s? (European settlers began to arrive.)

■ Name two ways that fishing was important to early colonists in the Northeast. (They used fish for food; Native Americans taught them how to use fish for plant fertilizer, which improved their crops.)

■ What do the cities of Salem, Boston, and Gloucester have in common? (All three are in Massachusetts and started out as fishing villages.)

■ What new tools have fishers learned to use over the years? (better boats, bigger nets, radios to communicate, sonar to locate fish)

Critical Thinking

■ Discuss with students why fish populations have declined in recent years. (overfishing) What can be done to address this problem? (Possible responses: The government can set limits on how many fish can be caught by individual fishers; catching certain kinds of fish can be made illegal.)

■ Ask students what new impressions they have about commercial fishers after reading the book. Would any students like to be commercial fishers? Why or why not?

FAST FACTS

■ Scientists have found fishhooks that date back 10,000 years, indicating that people fished thousands of years ago.

■ Many modern fishing boats use large nets called trawls, which drag along the ocean bottom to scoop up fish.

■ More fish are being caught than ever before. In 1965, about 60 million tons of fish were caught worldwide. In 1995, the figure had increased to 132 million tons.

■ To combat the depleted sources of fish in the world's oceans, some people have started fish farms.

■ People in the United States are eating more fish now than they have in the past. In 1980, the average person ate 12.5 pounds (5.67 kg) of fish a year. Twenty years later, the average person ate nearly 15 pounds (6.8 kg) of fish per year.

Activity

In Appreciation Of … : Invite students to design decoupage memorials to the fishers of the Northeast, using wood, paper cutouts, and shellac. Have students write short speeches to present as they unveil their memorials to the other members of the class.

Vocabulary

current: the movement of water in a river or an ocean

dory: a small boat used for fishing usually kept on a larger boat

fisher: a person who catches fish for a living or for sport

merchant ship: a ship that carries goods used for trade

plankton: animals and plants, usually tiny, that drift or float in oceans and lakes

sonar: an instrument used to determine where underwater objects are by sending sound waves through the water and listening as they bounce back; *sonar* stands for *s*ound *na*vigation *r*anging.

weir: a fishing device used by Native Americans to corral fish into an enclosed area

EXTENSION ACTIVITIES

FISHING, YESTERDAY AND TODAY

Curriculum Area: Social Studies
Skills: Comparing and Contrasting, Making Inferences, Noticing Details

Have students review the photographs in the Reader that show what fishing was like long ago for Native American people and what it is like for professional fishers today. Then distribute copies of page 15, which explores the ways in which fishing has changed over the past 500 years. After completing the activity, students may create posters that describe and illustrate what they have learned.

LOST AT SEA

Curriculum Area: Language Arts
Skill: Creative Writing

Ask students to recall the dangers many fishers face when fishing the North Atlantic. Talk about the fierce weather and the debilitating fogs. Suggest that such a setting would be perfect for an adventure story. Invite students to write stories with ocean settings. Choose several stories to read aloud to the class

ANSWER KEY

COPYING MASTERS

Page 15 Part I: 1. b, **2.** d, **3.** a, **4.** c

Part II: Possible Responses: **1.** Today's nets scoop up entire schools of fish. **2.** The use of radios helps fishers communicate with each other. **3.** Sonar helps fishers find fish by reflecting back soundwaves underwater. **4.** Today's ships are bigger, sturdier, and more powerful than ships of yesterday.

Part III: Possible responses: Today's methods are better because they allow fishers to catch more fish; past methods were better because the fish remained plentiful.

Page 16 1. True; **2.** False: Grand Bank is off the coast of Canada. **3.** False: The first people to fish off the coast of North America were Native Americans. **4.** False: John Cabot was impressed with the amount of fish and described his findings to people back in Britain. **5.** True; **6.** False: The National Marine Fisheries Service found that during a four-year span the fish population had decreased by more than half.

READER

Think and Respond 1. Positive: More fish can be caught. Negative: Seas are being overfished. **2.** The Gulf Stream, which flows past the coast, is warm and carries lots of plankton, making this region a feeding and breeding ground for all kinds of fish. **3.** wooden spears, hooks made from animal bones, nets made from plant fibers; **4.** Have communications devices and life vests on board; follow weather forecasts; fish with a partner.

Write a Description Students' descriptions should include specific information and details from the Reader.

Name _____

Fishing, Yesterday and Today

Part I Long ago, Native Americans used simple but effective tools for catching fish. Match the tool with the animal or plant part from which it was made.

1. fish hooks   a. plant fibers
2. spears   b. animal bones
3. fishing line and nets   c. tree shoots
4. weirs   d. wood

Part II What do you know about fishing today? Explain how each item listed below helps today's fishers catch fish.

nets _____

_____

radio _____

_____

sonar _____

_____

ships _____

_____

Part III Which fishing methods do you think are better—those of yesterday or those of today? Explain your opinion with evidence from the book.

_____

_____

_____

_____

_____

_____

© Harcourt

Fishing Statements— True or False?

Read the statements below. Decide if each is true or false. If the statement is true, write **true**. If the statement is false, rewrite it to make it true.

1. Strong ocean currents create just the right conditions for many kinds of fish in North Atlantic waters. True or false?

_____

_____

_____

2. Georges Bank is off the coast of Cape Cod, and Grand Bank is off the coast of Gloucester. True or false?

_____

_____

_____

3. The first people to fish off the coast of North America were the Portuguese. True or false?

_____

_____

_____

4. John Cabot was disappointed in the amount of fish he saw off the North American coast when he arrived from Britain. True or false?

_____

_____

_____

5. The most abundant fish to catch in North Atlantic waters used to be the cod. True or false?

_____

_____

_____

6. A survey counted by the National Marine Fisheries Service found that fish populations were not decreasing in the 1990s but were actually increasing. True or false?

_____

_____

_____

Bonus: Write your own True/False statements, based on what you've learned from *A Fisher's Life.* Try to stump your classmates!

_____

_____

_____

_____

_____

A FISHER'S LIFE

The Pine Barrens

BACKGROUND

Summary

Although the impression many people might have of New Jersey is of a state filled with factories, highways, and buildings, nearly a quarter of the state is open land. One open area is the Pine Barrens in southern New Jersey. Here, more than 1.1 million acres, plants and animals thrive in a unique ecosystem.

READING TIPS

Building Background

■ Invite a student volunteer to locate the state of New Jersey on a classroom map. Have students locate major cities in New Jersey (Newark, Atlantic City, Trenton, and Camden) and the surrounding metropolitan areas (New York and Philadelphia).

■ Ask students to share their impressions of New Jersey. What images come to mind when they think of this state? After eliciting ideas, have a volunteer read the first paragraph of the book. Compare students' initial ideas with this description.

Reading for Details

■ How large is the Pinelands National Reserve? (1.1 million acres)

■ How long have human beings occupied the Pine Barrens? (more than 10,000 years)

■ How did the Pine Barrens get its name? (European settlers considered the lands, although covered with pine trees, to be mostly barren.)

■ What is significant about the year 1840 in the Pine Barrens' history? (The first cranberry bog was made in 1840. Since then, New Jersey has become the third biggest producer of cranberries in the United States.)

■ Why is the water that flows through the Pine Barrens brown? (The color comes from the roots and bark of cedar trees.)

■ What threats do endangered plants and animals face in the Pine Barrens? (floods, droughts, fires, human interference)

■ How does fire help the Pine Barrens? (During a fire, the cones of the pitch pine open, allowing the cones to drop their seeds and ensuring that more plants will grow.)

Critical Thinking

■ After reading the book, invite students to share new ideas or impressions about New Jersey. Encourage them to write descriptive sentences about the state, referring not only to its industrial cities but also to its wild Pine Barrens.

■ Ask students if they would like to visit the Pine Barrens. Encourage them to recall the

FAST FACTS

■ One can drive through or beside the Pine Barrens on the Garden State Parkway, which runs over 160 miles (257 km) from the northern end of New Jersey to the southern tip.

■ Along with farming and recreation, activities in the Pine Barrens include harvesting shellfish and extracting resources, mainly sand and gravel.

■ Scientists have found more than 1,000 prehistoric sites in the Pine Barrens, some dating back more than 10,000 years.

■ The Lenape Indians were early residents of the Pine Barrens. They left the area after the arrival of European settlers, who drew upon the Pine Barrens' many natural resources, including timber and iron ore.

■ A total of 54 plants and 39 animals that are threatened with extinction in New Jersey are found in the Pine Barrens.

■ Places to visit in the New Jersey Pine Barrens include Barnegat Lighthouse State Park, Lebanon State Forest, and Double Trouble State Park.

special features that make the Pine Barrens unique and interesting.

Activity

■ **Who Needs the Pine Barrens?:** Ask students to imagine that a major land developer has offered the state of New Jersey a large sum of money to purchase the Pine Barrens. The developer wishes to cut down the trees, drain the swampland, and build shopping malls and neighborhoods there. Have students list the pros and cons of such an endeavor. Should the state of New Jersey accept the developer's offer? Why or why not?

Vocabulary

aquifer: rock or soil that is able to store water

biosphere reserve: a protected area with an unusual ecosystem, surrounded by an area that is less protected

ecosystem: a community of animals and plants interacting with their environment

endangered species: a type of plant or animal that is in danger of becoming extinct

natural habitat: the place and conditions in nature in which a plant or an animal lives

natural resource: a material found in nature that is necessary or useful to people

reservoir: a holding area for storing a large amount of water

smelt: to melt ore so that the metal can be removed

water table: the top of an underground area that is full of water

wildlife: wild animals living in their natural environment

EXTENSION ACTIVITIES

LOOKING AT PHOTOGRAPHS

Curriculum Area: Science/Ecology
Skills: Observation, Critical Thinking,
     Comparing and Contrasting

Invite students to study the photographs of the Pine Barrens throughout the book and to try to identify the animals and plants they see. Then have students compare the Pine Barrens with a natural setting in their own community. How is the landscape similar or different? How are the plants similar or different? The animals? The natural features? Have students

represent the similarities and differences in a two-column chart or Venn diagram.

PINE BARRENS CAUSE AND EFFECT

Curriculum Area: Science/Ecology
Skills: Recognizing Cause and Effect, Drawing Conclusions,
     Summarizing, Diagramming

Distribute copies of page 19. Discuss the chain of causes and effects listed in the left-hand column. Point out that in an ecosystem, one event can cause something to change, which in turn causes something else to change, and so on. Review some simple cause-and-effect scenarios from the book. For example, the Lenape Indians came into contact with European settlers (cause), and many Lenapes became ill from European diseases (effect). Then challenge students to complete the chart on the right-hand side of the handout, drawing on information presented in the book.

- -
ANSWER KEY
- -

COPYING MASTERS

Page 19 Effect/Cause: Too much water will be pumped up. **Effect/Cause:** The water table will sink. **Effect:** The sinking water table will harm the plants and animals that need it to stay at a certain level.

Page 20 Students' word choices should be grammatically and semantically appropriate.

READER

Think and Respond 1. cranberries and blueberries; **2.** pollutants such as pesticides and fertilizers, overbuilding in the surrounding region; **3.** uplands and lowlands, a mix of trees, sandy soil; **4.** Possible response: yes, in order to share these spaces with people in the future, to prevent the extinction of animals and plants, and to protect the health of the natural environment

Research and Present Students' presentations should describe the history and development of the park.

Name_____

A Sensitive Ecosystem: Cause and Effect

Many events can affect the delicate ecosystem of the Pine Barrens. After reviewing with your teacher the information in the left-hand column, fill in the right-hand column with information about the cause-and-effect relationships you read about in the book.

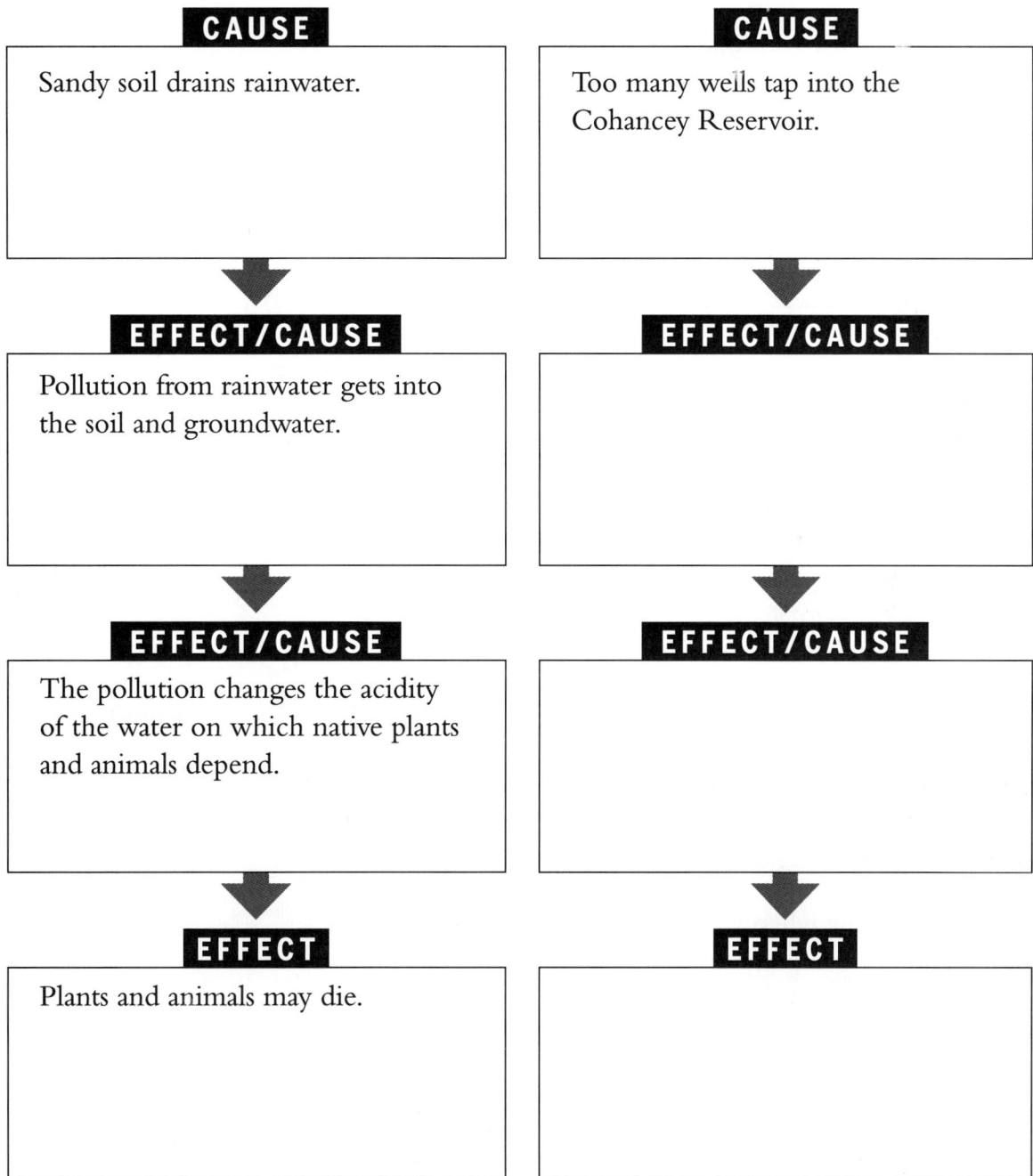

CAUSE

Sandy soil drains rainwater.

CAUSE

Too many wells tap into the Cohancey Reservoir.

EFFECT/CAUSE

Pollution from rainwater gets into the soil and groundwater.

EFFECT/CAUSE

EFFECT/CAUSE

The pollution changes the acidity of the water on which native plants and animals depend.

EFFECT/CAUSE

EFFECT

Plants and animals may die.

EFFECT

Pine Barrens Nature Walk

Imagine you've just taken a nature walk through the Pine Barrens.
Write an e-mail message to a friend describing what you saw and did.
Fill in the paragraphs below with words that tell about the Pine Barrens.
The type of word you need is written below each blank.

Dear _____ ,
        (name)

    I took the most _____ nature hike in the Pine Barrens of New Jersey!
        (adjective)

The animals were _____ . I saw a(n) _____ ,
            (adjective)   *(animal name)*

a(n) _____ , and a(n) _____ .
     (animal name)   *(animal name)*

I feel so _____ for these creatures because their habitat is so
     (emotion)

_____ . I also saw many plants, such as
   (adjective)

_____ , _____ , and _____ .
  (plant name)   *(plant name)*   *(plant name)*

    To tell the truth, when I saw the Pine Barrens for the first time, I felt

_____ . There didn't seem to be too much to the Pine Barrens. But
  (emotion)

when you _____ more closely, you can see just how _____
      (verb)   *(adjective)*

the wildlife and plants are.

    Some people want to _____ the Pine Barrens. I think this is a
                 (verb)

_____ idea. Once you _____ the Pine Barrens, you'll
  (adjective)   *(verb)*

want to _____ this _____ land, too.
     (verb)   *(adjective)*

    Let me know when you'll be visiting, and we'll _____ the
                                   (verb)

Pine Barrens together!

        Your friend,

        _____
            (your name)

TIME FOR KIDS READERS
It Happened at Seneca Falls

BACKGROUND

Summary

Less than a century ago, women in the United States were not able to do something that many women around the world can do today—they were not allowed to vote. In 1920, American women were finally granted the right to vote. The fight for woman suffrage had begun decades earlier in Seneca Falls, New York.

READING TIPS

Building Background

■ Why is the right to vote important to United States citizens? (Voting allows all citizens to participate in decisions that affect their nation, their communities, and their individual lives.)

FAST FACTS

■ In 1789 the United States Constitution established voting guidelines that left to the states the decision of who should be allowed to vote. Most states extended voting privileges only to white male property owners.

■ The Nineteenth Amendment to the United States Constitution granted women the right to vote.

■ The four women most often associated with the suffrage movement are Susan B. Anthony, Elizabeth Blackwell, Carrie Chapman Catt, Lucretia Mott, and Elizabeth Cady Stanton.

■ Some men, including abolitionist Frederick Douglass and poet Ralph Waldo Emerson, also supported the woman suffrage movement.

■ In July 1848 a church in Seneca Falls, New York, was the site of the first organized convention to discuss woman suffrage.

■ If you were an adult citizen, how would you feel if you were denied the right to vote? (Possible responses: angry, frustrated, powerless)

Reading for Details

■ What were some of the things women were not allowed to do in the mid-1800s? (Women were not allowed to vote, to own property, to attend most colleges, or to have certain careers.)
■ How many people attended the convention in Seneca Falls, New York? (approximately 300)
■ Who ran the meeting in Seneca Falls? (Lucretia Mott's husband, James)
■ Which formerly enslaved African American man spoke in support of women's right to vote? (Frederick Douglass)
■ Why was Susan B. Anthony arrested in 1872? (because she voted in the Presidential election)
■ What Constitutional amendment was introduced in Congress each year, starting in 1878? (a woman suffrage amendment)
■ If the House of Representatives and the Senate passed the Nineteenth Amendment in 1919, why wasn't the amendment made into law until 1920? (In order for an amendment to become law, it must be approved by two-thirds or more of the states after it has been passed by Congress.)

Critical Thinking

■ Why do you think so many people objected to the idea of giving women the right to vote? (Possible responses: concern that women weren't intelligent enough; fear that women would neglect their homes and children if they became involved in politics)
■ Do you think that men and women now have complete equality? Why or why not? (Possible responses: yes, because women can now vote, own property, attend college, and have many different kinds of careers; no, because some people still discriminate against women and many professions are still dominated by men)

Vocabulary

amendment: a change that is made to a law or a legal document

civil rights: the individual rights that all members of a society have, including the right to equal treatment under the law

conference: a formal meeting for discussing ideas and opinions

convention: a large gathering of people with the same interest

declaration: an announcement

defy: to refuse to obey

discrimination: prejudice or unjust behavior to others based on differences in age, race, gender, or other personal traits

opposition: being against something; a group that is against something

property: buildings or land belonging to someone

suffrage: the right to vote

EXTENSION ACTIVITIES

LOOKING AT PHOTOGRAPHS
Curriculum Area: Social Studies
Skills: Observation, Critical Thinking
Direct students' attention to pages 14 and 15 of the book, where they can see postage stamps honoring Elizabeth Cady Stanton, Carrie Chapman Catt, and Lucretia Mott. Ask: If you were to design a stamp in honor of a contemporary woman, whom would you choose?

NEWSWORTHY WOMEN
Curriculum Area: Language Arts
Skills: Recalling Facts, Categorizing Information, Expository Writing
The meeting in Seneca Falls was big news. Ask students to fill out the chart on page 23, referring to the book for information. Then challenge students to turn their notes into newspaper articles. Point out that the question words on the sheet—*who, what, where, when, why,* and *how*—cover the types of information reporters often include in news stories. When students have completed their articles, encourage them to copy them onto large sheets of newsprint to resemble a newspaper of the period.

GET OUT THE VOTE
Curriculum Areas: Social Studies, Language Arts, Art
Skills: Persuasive Writing, Graphic Design, Group Work
The right to vote has been hard-won in countries around the world—yet only about half of all adult Americans use it. Have students create posters designed to urge adults to vote. They might use the story of Seneca Falls and the woman suffrage movement to demonstrate the importance of voting rights. Have students bring in examples of actual posters and print ads to analyze their structure and format. Encourage them to use headlines, visuals, and persuasive writing techniques to convey their messages.

ANSWER KEY

COPYING MASTERS
Page 23 Who: Lucretia Mott, Cady Stanton, and approximately 300 other people; **What:** to discuss women's rights; **When:** July 19 and 20, 1848; **Where:** Wesleyan Chapel in Seneca Falls, New York; **Why:** Women were denied many rights that men had, such as the right to own property, to receive an education, to work in certain professions, and to vote; **How:** A notice was placed in the local paper, announcing the meeting.

Page 24 1. Seneca, **2.** suffrage, **3.** rights, opposition, **5.** property, Amendment
Mystery Person: Susan B. Anthony

READER
Think and Respond 1. Wyoming; **2.** The Nineteenth Amendment gives all U.S. citizens the right to vote, regardless of gender. **3.** 1920; **4.** Possible responses: Women could not vote; most jobs did not allow women; married women could not own property. **5.** Women are doctors, lawyers, governors, prime ministers, inventors, and athletes; modern women shape the world in which we live.

Give a Speech Students' speeches should include at least two reasons why the right to vote is important to all people.

Newsworthy Women

The meeting at Seneca Falls was big news. Fill out the reporter's log below with information from the book.

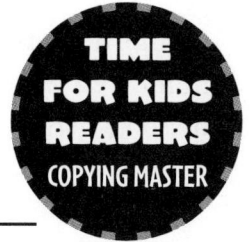

Who was at the meeting?

_____

_____

What was the meeting about?

_____

_____

When was the meeting held?

_____

_____

Where did the meeting take place?

_____

_____

Why was the meeting called?

_____

_____

How did people find out about the meeting?

_____

_____

_____

Use the facts from the chart to write a newspaper article about the meeting at Seneca Falls.

Name_____

Puzzle It Out

Complete each sentence with a word from the book. Write the numbered letters on the lines at the bottom to reveal the name of the mystery person.

Amendment
opposition
property
rights
Seneca
Suffrage

1. The first meeting to discuss women's rights was held in
___ ___ ___ ___ ___ ___ Falls, New York.
   3   6

2. ___ ___ ___ ___ ___ ___ ___ ___ means the right to vote.
    2

3. Civil ___ ___ ___ ___ ___ ___ include the right of all people to be treated
       9   1   equally under the law.

4. A group that is against something is called the
___ ___ ___ ___ ___ ___ ___ ___ ___ ___ .
      10   5

5. Two hundred years ago, women did not have the right to
own ___ ___ ___ ___ ___ ___ ___ ___ .
             8 12

6. The Nineteenth ___ ___ ___ ___ ___ ___ ___ ___ ___ gave women the right
to vote.   4   11   7

This woman, well-known for her work as a woman suffragist, was the first woman to appear on an American coin. Who was she?

___ ___ ___ ___ ___ B. ___ ___ ___ ___ ___ ___ ___
 1 2 3 4 5   6 7 8 9 10 11 12

The Cajuns

BACKGROUND

Summary

The Cajun people have a history that extends far beyond their current location in New Orleans, Louisiana. Originally called Acadians, these early French settlers once lived in the area of Canada that is now called Nova Scotia. Forced to leave when the British won the right to rule the Canadian region, many Acadians settled in the southern United States. Their history is one of heartbreak and endurance.

READING TIPS

Building Background

■ Write the word *Cajun* on the chalkboard. Invite students to share the images that come to mind when they hear this word. Create a word web by circling the word *Cajun* and jotting down students' ideas in smaller circles around it.

■ Ask students if they know where Cajun people originated. Have them locate France on a map and trace a route across the Atlantic Ocean from France to Nova Scotia. Then have them trace a route from Nova Scotia down along the Atlantic coast to Louisiana. Allow students to speculate about why a group of people might have journeyed so far.

Reading for Details

■ What type of life did the French ancestors of the Cajuns have in France? (They were poor farmers.) Why did they leave France to travel to North America? (They were looking for a better life.)

■ What does the term *La Cadie* mean in Micmac? ("land of plenty")

■ How were the settlers' lives in Nova Scotia better than they had been in France? (Possible responses: Food was plentiful; they had more freedoms; they could be independent; they were healthy; they appeared to enjoy their simple life.)

■ Why did Acadian people leave Nova Scotia? (The British took control of the region and forced them to leave.)

■ Why was their leaving called the Great Upheaval? (*An upheaval* is a sudden upset or disturbance, which is what the Acadians experienced when they were forced to leave.)

■ What is the ancestry of Creole people? (They are descendants of the original French settlers of Louisiana.)

■ How were Cajuns different from the rest of the people of Louisiana? (They lived in the backwoods, away from most people, and spoke Cajun French instead of English.)

FAST FACTS

■ The Cajun people of Louisiana share common roots with Canadians of French descent.

■ The original Acadians were French settlers who immigrated to North America in the early 1600s.

■ At a dig in Nova Scotia, archaeologists found a number of Acadian artifacts—including mugs, bowls, bottles, plates, jars, buckles, buttons, and coins—that date from the 1670s.

■ The British won the right to rule the Canadian region as a result of the French and Indian War of 1754–1763. The Treaty of Paris, signed at the end of the war, gave Acadian people 18 months to relocate to France.

■ Historians estimate that of the 12,000 Acadians forced to leave Nova Scotia, 2,500 to 3,000 ended up in Louisiana, which was a French colony at the time.

■ According to the 1990 United States census, almost 600,000 U.S. residents are of Acadian/Cajun ancestry and more than 1.5 million are of French Canadian ancestry.

Critical Thinking

■ Talk with students about the Great Upheaval. Do they think it was right for the British to force the Acadians to leave? How might the British have handled this situation differently? (Possible responses: The British could have given the Acadians more time to prepare for departure; they could have made sure that families were not separated from each other; they could have provided the Acadians with a safer means of travel; they could have allowed the Acadians to stay.)

Activity

■ **Before and After:** Have students compare the lives of the Acadians in Nova Scotia with the lives of their Cajun descendants in Louisiana. How were their lives similar? How were they different? Have students work in groups to represent their ideas in a two-column chart or Venn diagram.

Vocabulary

backwoods: an area with a lot of forest but very few people

bayou: a stream that runs slowly through a swamp and leads to or from a lake or river

frontier: the far edge of a country, where few people live

indentured servant: a person who agrees to work for someone else without pay for a fixed period of time

territory: a region

upheaval: a sudden and violent upset or disturbance

zydeco: a form of music with roots in African American and Creole culture

EXTENSION ACTIVITIES

SURVIVING THE GREAT UPHEAVAL

Curriculum Areas: Social Studies, Language Arts
Skills: Recalling Information, Understanding Historical
       Perspective, Creative Writing

Ask students to imagine what it might have been like for the Acadians of Nova Scotia to be uprooted from their homes in the1870s. After discussing the Great Upheaval, invite students to write three journal entries in which they reflect on this experience from the perspective of a displaced Acadian person. Journal entries should focus on life in Nova Scotia, the hardship of moving, and settlement in the new region.

CAJUN CULTURE FESTIVAL

Curriculum Areas: Social Studies, Language Arts, Art
Skills: Research, Organization, Cooperative Learning,
       Oral Presentation

Divide the class into groups, and assign each group one of the following topics: New Orleans Today, Cajun Food, Cajun Music, Cajun Arts and Crafts, and the Ecosystem of the Louisiana Bayou. Ask the groups to research their topics and to think of creative ways to share information with the class. Make time in your schedule for a Cajun Culture Festival, at which students can present what they learned to their classmates and other invited guests.

ANSWER KEY

COPYING MASTERS

Page 27 The correct sequence is b, d, a, f, c, e.

Page 28 1. Creoles, **2.** Micmac, **3.** hunger, **4.** Zydeco, **5.** bayou, **6.** French, **7.** po' boy, **8.** jambalaya, **9.** Upheaval, **10.** frontier, **11.** British, **12.** Maryland; **Hidden Phrase:** land of plenty

READER

Think and Respond **1.** France; **2.** Possible responses: The Louisiana Territory allowed the Cajuns to enjoy fishing and hunting; they could cultivate their own land. **3.** music: zydeco; food: gumbo, Jambalaya, po' boys; **4.** Students may choose from Cajun musical instruments such as fiddles, guitars, accordions, washboards, triangles, and spoons.

Write a Description Students' descriptions should include specific details about their families' culinary and musical traditions, including a description of the events at which these traditions may be found.

Tracking History

The events below tell the history of the Cajun people, but they are out of order. What happened first? What happened next? Write the letter of each event in a box on the time line to show the correct sequence.

a. Acadian people lead a simple life in Nova Scotia.

b. The ancestors of the Acadians live as poor farmers in France.

c. The Acadians are forced to leave Canada.

d. The Acadians settle in Nova Scotia.

e. Acadians gather in Louisiana, where they develop the Cajun culture.

f. The British gain control of Canada.

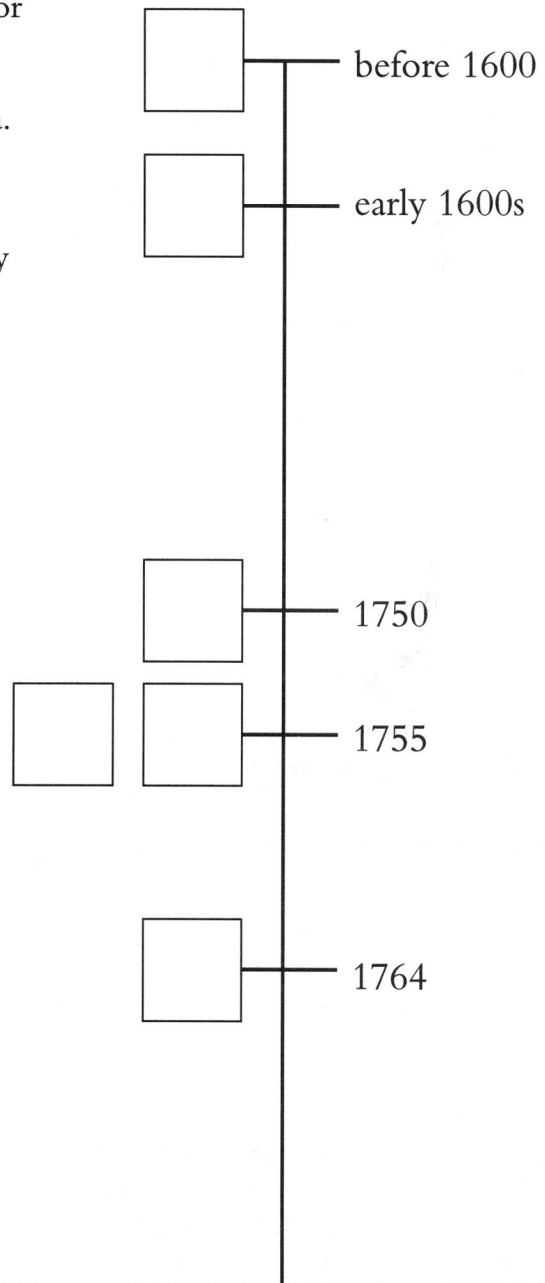

before 1600

early 1600s

1750

1755

1764

What Does It Mean?

The word *Cajun* comes from the word *Acadia,* which comes from the Native American term *La Cadie.* To find out what this term means, use the clues to fill in the words in the puzzle below. Then look at the letters in the boxes. What do they spell?

1. The children of Louisiana's early French settlers were called

___ ___ ___ ___ ◯ ___ ___.

2. Which language does *La Cadie* come from? ___ ___ ___ ___ ◯ ___

3. On the ships that carried the Acadians away from Nova Scotia, most people died from smallpox and ___ ___ ◯ ___ ___ ___ .

4. ___ ___ ◯ ___ ___ ___ is a form of music that mixes African American and Creole influences.

5. Swampy land in Louisiana is called a ___ ___ ___ ◯ ___ .

6. Which nationality were Cajun and Acadian people originally?

◯ ___ ___ ___ ___ ___

7. A Cajun catfish sandwich is called a ◯ ___' ___ ___ ___ .

8. Rice mixed with shrimp, chicken, and other meat is called

___ ___ ___ ___ ___ ◯ ___ ___ ___ .

9. The forced departure of the Acadians from Nova Scotia is known as the Great

___ ___ ___ ◯ ___ ___ ___ ___ ___ .

10. An area in which only a few settlers live is called the

___ ___ ___ ◯ ___ ___ ___ ___ .

11. The ___ ___ ___ ◯ ___ ___ ___ made the Acadians leave Nova Scotia.

12. Which was the only state that treated the displaced Acadians kindly?

___ ___ ___ ◯ ___ ___ ___ ___

Hidden Phrase:

___ ___ ___ ___ ___ ___ ___ ___ ___ ___ ___ ___

THE CAJUNS

At the Center of the Earth

BACKGROUND

Summary

One of the world's biggest caves is right here in the United States. Mammoth Cave in Kentucky lives up to its name: its passageways stretch some 348 miles (560 km) and its depths reach approximately 379 feet (116 m). The mystery of the cave has lured many explorers to discover its dark interior. Today, people can travel through the cave on designated paths to marvel at the natural wonders within.

READING TIPS

Building Background

■ Invite students to share their ideas about caves. Challenge them to come up with specific adjectives to describe caves. (Possible responses: spooky, eerie, dark, mysterious) What, if anything, could they see inside a cave? What sounds would they hear? What would a cave smell like? How would the air in a cave feel?

■ Ask students what they know about cave exploration. Why do people explore caves? (Possible responses: for fun or excitement; in order to learn more about Earth's structure)

FAST FACTS

■ Mammoth Cave became part of the United States National Park System in 1941.

■ Mammoth Cave National Park sits on 52,830 acres and includes forests and rivers as well as the cave.

■ Other cave systems in Kentucky include Carter Caves State Park, Kentucky Caverns, Crystal Onyx Cave, and Diamond Caverns.

■ *A spelunker* is a person who explores caves.

Reading for Details

■ To what does the author compare warm water dripping on an ice cube? (The author compares the holes the warm water makes on the ice cube's surface to the holes falling rain makes on the earth's surface.)

■ In what part of Kentucky is Mammoth Cave? (south-central Kentucky)

■ How much bigger is Mammoth Cave than Optimisticeskaya Cave in the Ukraine? (234 miles [377 km] longer and 313 feet [95 m] deeper)

■ How long does it take a cave to form? (A cave can take hundreds, thousands, or even millions of years to form.)

■ How can we tell that people explored Mammoth Cave thousands of years ago? (Cave explorers today have found ancient torches, wall paintings, and even human bones.)

■ Who was Stephen Bishop? (He was an enslaved African who led tours of the cave, which was on his master's lands. He began exploring the cave on his own, going into places where no one else had yet gone.)

■ When did Mammoth Cave become an official national park of the United States? (1941)

Critical Thinking

■ Recall the story of Floyd Collins. Ask: Is cave exploration worth the risks it involves? Encourage students to think of other dangerous sports or hobbies, such as mountain climbing, rock climbing, and race-car driving. Why are some people attracted to these kinds of activities?

Activity

■ **Come In!** Stephen Bishop's enthusiasm for Mammoth Cave made him an excellent tour guide. Have students work in groups to create a short speech that Bishop might have given to a tour group. What interesting details or stories would he have included in order to capture his listeners' attention? Encourage students to make the speeches full of energy and excitement so that they convey Bishop's love of the cave. Then invite one member of each group to present the speech as they imagine Bishop might have done.

Vocabulary

biosphere reserve: a protected area of land with an unusual ecosystem, surrounded by an area that is less protected

crystal: a clear or nearly clear mineral or rock

gypsum: a white mineral that is used to make plaster of Paris

limestone: a hard rock formed from the remains of shells or coral

mineral: a substance found in nature that is not an animal or a plant

natural wonder: something that occurs in nature that inspires awe

predicament: an awkward or difficult situation

spire: a structure that comes to a point at the top

stalactite: a thin piece of rock shaped like an icicle that hangs from the roof of a cave

stalagmite: a thin piece of rock shaped like an icicle that sticks up from the floor of a cave

tourist: someone who travels and visits places for pleasure

EXTENSION ACTIVITIES

LEGENDS OF THE CAVE

Curriculum Area: Language Arts
Skills: Applying Knowledge, Understanding Story Elements, Pre-writing, Creative Writing

Invite a volunteer to read the section of the book that tells the story of the discovery of Mammoth Cave by a man named Houchins. Point out that the author refers to this as "one popular story." Speculate with students about other possible stories. Then encourage them to write their own legends about Mammoth Cave's discovery. Distribute copies of page 31. Review the elements of a story. Instruct students to use the map to plan their stories and to refer to it as they write their first drafts. Publish the legends in a class anthology.

CAVE EXPLORERS

Curriculum Areas: Science, Art
Skills: Applying Knowledge, Making Inferences, Small-Motor Skills, Visualizing

Ask students to imagine that they are cave explorers. While exploring Mammoth Cave, they stumble upon a new cavern within the cave. What is this cavern like? What cave features does it have? What would they name it? What would they tell tourists about it? Then invite students to make dioramas representing their caves. Have students bring in shoe boxes from home, supply them with art materials, and invite them to create their imaginary caves inside the box. To accompany their dioramas, ask students to write a paragraph that explains the cave, its features, and how the students "discovered" it. Display the dioramas around the room.

ANSWER KEY

COPYING MASTERS

Page 31 Students' stories should include a clearly defined main character, conflict, rising action, climax, resolution, and appropriate details about caves.

Page 32 Troglobites: flatworms, eyeless fish, millipedes; Troglophiles: worms, snails, spiders; Trogloxenes: bats, crickets, pack rats; Incidentals: frogs, raccoons, humans

READER

Think and Respond 1. Troglobites are cave dwellers; troglophiles are cave lovers; trogloxenes are cave guests. **2.** Rainwater hits Earth's surface and mixes with bits of limestone, which makes the water more acidic; over millions of years, this acidic water wears away Earth's surface. **3.** The U.S. government wanted to protect the cave's wildlife and natural features. **4.** Limestone makes rainwater acidic. **5.** Students should give specific reasons to support their opinions.

Research and Mapping Cave locations should be clearly marked and labeled on students' world maps.

Name _____

Legends of the Cave

How do you think Mammoth Cave might have been discovered?
Use the story map below to plan your story. Refer to the map as you
write your story on a separate sheet of paper.

Character:
Who is the main character? What is he or she like?

Conflict: What problem does
the main character face?

Rising Action: How does the
character try to solve the problem?

Climax: At what point do the
conflict and action reach the
highest peak?

Resolution: How does the main
character solve the problem?

© Harcourt

Life in a Cave

Four types of animals can be found in Mammoth Cave: troglobites, troglophiles, trogloxenes, and incidentals. Read the list of animals below. Then write the name of each animal in the correct section of the chart.

raccoons	crickets	eyeless fish
bats	spiders	pack rats
flatworms	humans	frogs
snails	millipedes	worms

Troglobites

Troglophiles

Trogloxenes

Incidentals

Sites of the Civil War

BACKGROUND

Summary

Every year, millions of people visit battlefields on which the Civil War unfolded. Visiting these sites lends a sense of immediacy to one of the most compelling chapters in United States history. Adjacent parks, monuments, museums, bookstores, and guided tours teach valuable lessons about the "War Between the States" and the people who fought it.

READING TIPS

Building Background

■ Ask students what they know about the Civil War. Create a large chart with several headings (for example, Reasons, Famous People, Battles, Effects) and record students' ideas in the appropriate columns. Display the chart so students can confirm or revise their ideas as they read the book.

FAST FACTS

■ The Civil War, also called the War Between the States or the War for Southern Independence, lasted from 1861 to 1865.

■ The two opposing sides of the war were the Northern states, or the Union, and the Southern states, or the Confederacy.

■ The war developed because leaders in the Southern states wanted to secede, or break away, from the United States to form their own nation.

■ One of the key issues of the war was slavery. Most plantation owners in the Southern states relied heavily on the labor of enslaved persons. Many people in the North believed that slavery should be abolished.

■ The Civil War caused $5 billion worth of property damage and cost more than 600,000 lives.

Reading for Details

■ What is significant about the date April 12, 1861? (This is the day the Civil War began, at Fort Sumter, South Carolina.)

■ Why is Richmond, Virginia, called "the other capital?" (It was the capital of the Confederacy, or the Southern states, during the Civil War.)

■ Which battle is considered "the worst day" in Civil War history and why? (the battle at Antietam, Maryland, because after it 23,000 men were dead, wounded, or missing)

■ Which battle is often considered the turning point of the war? (the battle at Gettysburg, which the Union army won)

■ Which was the last Confederate-held city on the Mississippi, and what happened there? (Vicksburg was captured by the Union army led by Ulysses S. Grant.)

■ What is significant about Appomattox Court House in Virginia? (It is the place where Lee signed the Confederates' surrender, ending the war.)

Critical Thinking

■ Have students recall some important Civil War figures mentioned in the book. (Possible responses: John Brown, Jefferson Davis, Frederick Douglass, Ulysses S. Grant, Robert E. Lee, Abraham Lincoln) Who do they feel had the most influence? Why?

■ Invite students to express how they feel about the Civil War. Talk about the issues involved as well as the number of lives lost. Discuss if students think the war was necessary. Was there any other way to resolve the conflict?

Activity

■ **Rallying the Troops:** Speeches were one way that Civil War generals encouraged their troops before each battle. Ask students to speculate on what a general might say in such a speech. Work as a class to create a speech, going around the room round-robin style, asking each student to contribute a line. Let student volunteers take turns presenting the speech to the rest of the class.

Vocabulary

abolitionist: someone who worked to put an end to slavery before the Civil War

blockade: to close off an area to keep people or supplies from going in or out

Confederacy: the Southern states

entrenchment: a hole or trench soldiers dig for defense

foe: enemy

memorial: something that helps people continue to remember a person or an event

morale: the state of mind or spirit of a person or group

provisions: a supply of groceries or food

shell: a metal or paper case that hold's bullet and it's explosive

Union: the Northern states

EXTENSION ACTIVITIES

LOOKING AT ILLUSTRATIONS

Curriculum Area: Social Studies
Skills: Observation, Critical Thinking

Divide the class into groups and ask each group to select an illustration from the book to study, using the following questions as a guide: What details can you see in the picture? What do you notice about the people or the setting? What can this illustration teach about the Civil War and the people who took part in it?

WHERE IN THE UNION . . . OR CONFEDERACY?

Curriculum Area: Social Studies/Geography
Skills: Listening, Skimming for Information, Map Skills, Group Work

Divide the class into groups and distribute copies of page 35. Tell students that the map on this page will serve as the board for a game they are about to play. Explain that you are going to say a number, followed by the name of a battle or battlefield. (See Answer Key for list of battles and locations.) Students must figure out in which state each battle took place and write the number of the battle in the

empty square in that state. After reading each clue, give students a few minutes to find the answer in the book or to discuss the answer with their teammates. The team that locates the most battles correctly wins.

ODE TO THE CIVIL WAR

Curriculum Area: Language Arts
Skill: Creative Writing

Write the letters of "T-H-E C-I-V-I-L W-A-R" vertically on the chalkboard. Ask students to do the same on sheets of writing paper. They should have 11 letters written on 11 lines. Challenge students, working individually or in pairs, to compose Civil War poems, using a different letter from the phrase "The Civil War" to start each line. Tell them that their poems can rhyme, but they don't have to. Encourage students to express not only the events of the Civil War but also their own thoughts and feelings about it. Have students share their poems with the class. Then collect them in a class Civil War poetry anthology.

ANSWER KEY

COPYING MASTERS

Page 36 1. Fort Sumter (South Carolina), **2.** Manassas (Virginia), **3.** Shiloh (Tennessee), **4.** Antietam (Maryland), **5.** Gettysburg (Pennsylvania), **6.** Vicksburg (Mississippi), **7.** Atlanta (Georgia)

Page 37 ACROSS: 3. Davis, **4.** Douglass, **9.** Rosecrans, **10.** Brown, **11.** Lee; **DOWN: 1.** Jackson, **2.** Thomas, **5.** Lincoln, **6.** Sherman, **7.** McClellan, **8.** Grant

READER

Think and Respond 1. Washington, D.C.; **2.** Possible responses: it was a war in which Americans fought Americans; the war was fought over issues that still affect us today. **3.** Possible responses: It was a turning point in the war; the Confederates were defeated and retreated to Virginia; more than 51,000 men were killed. **4.** Students should give specific reasons to support their opinions.

Create a Time Line Students' time lines should be in chronological order and be accurately labeled.

Where in the Union— or Confederacy?

Listen to the names of the battles your teacher reads.
Write the number of the battle in the correct state.

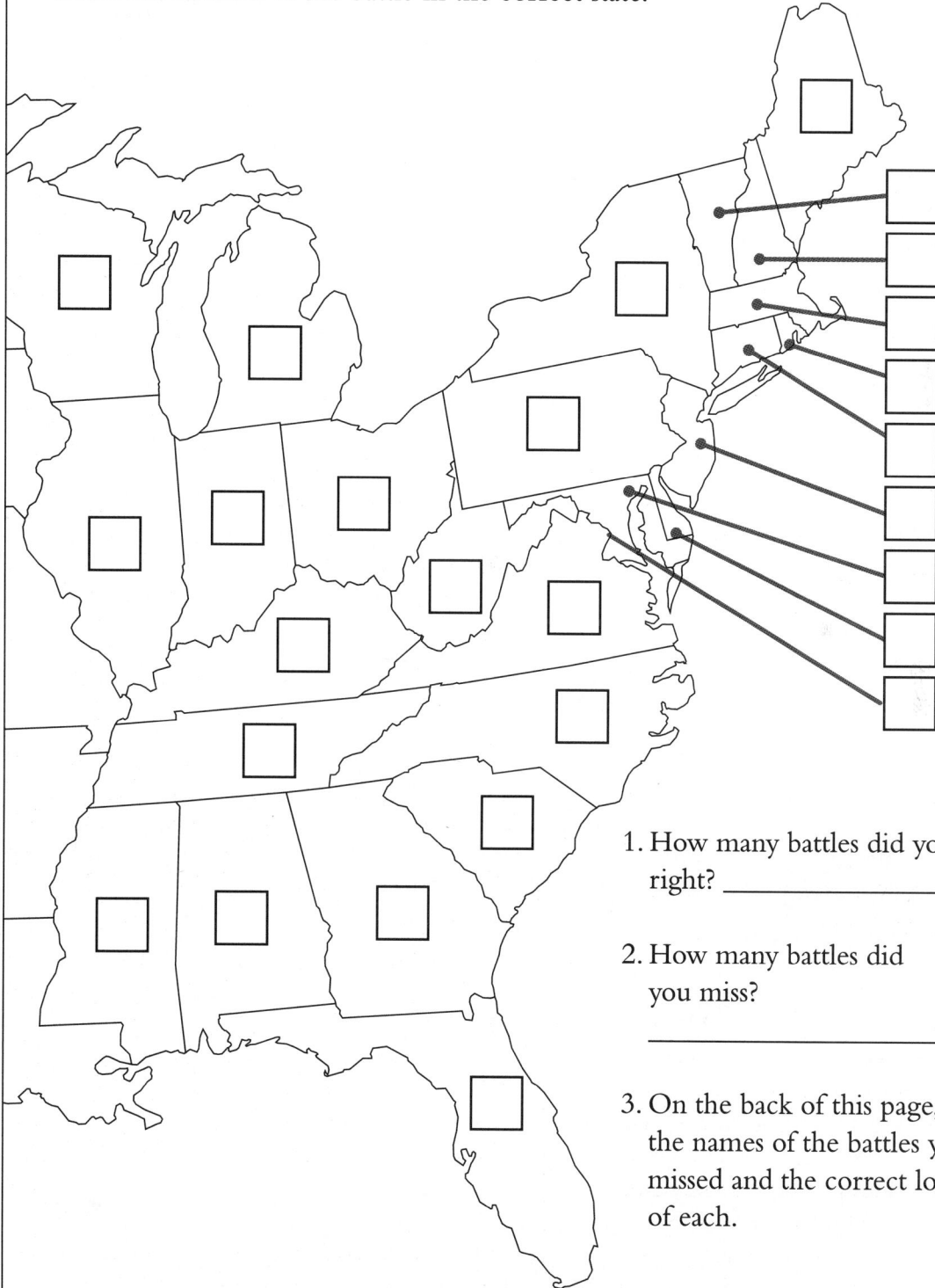

1. How many battles did you get right? _____

2. How many battles did you miss?

_____

3. On the back of this page, write the names of the battles you missed and the correct location of each.

Figures of the Civil War

Complete each sentence and write the name in the puzzle.

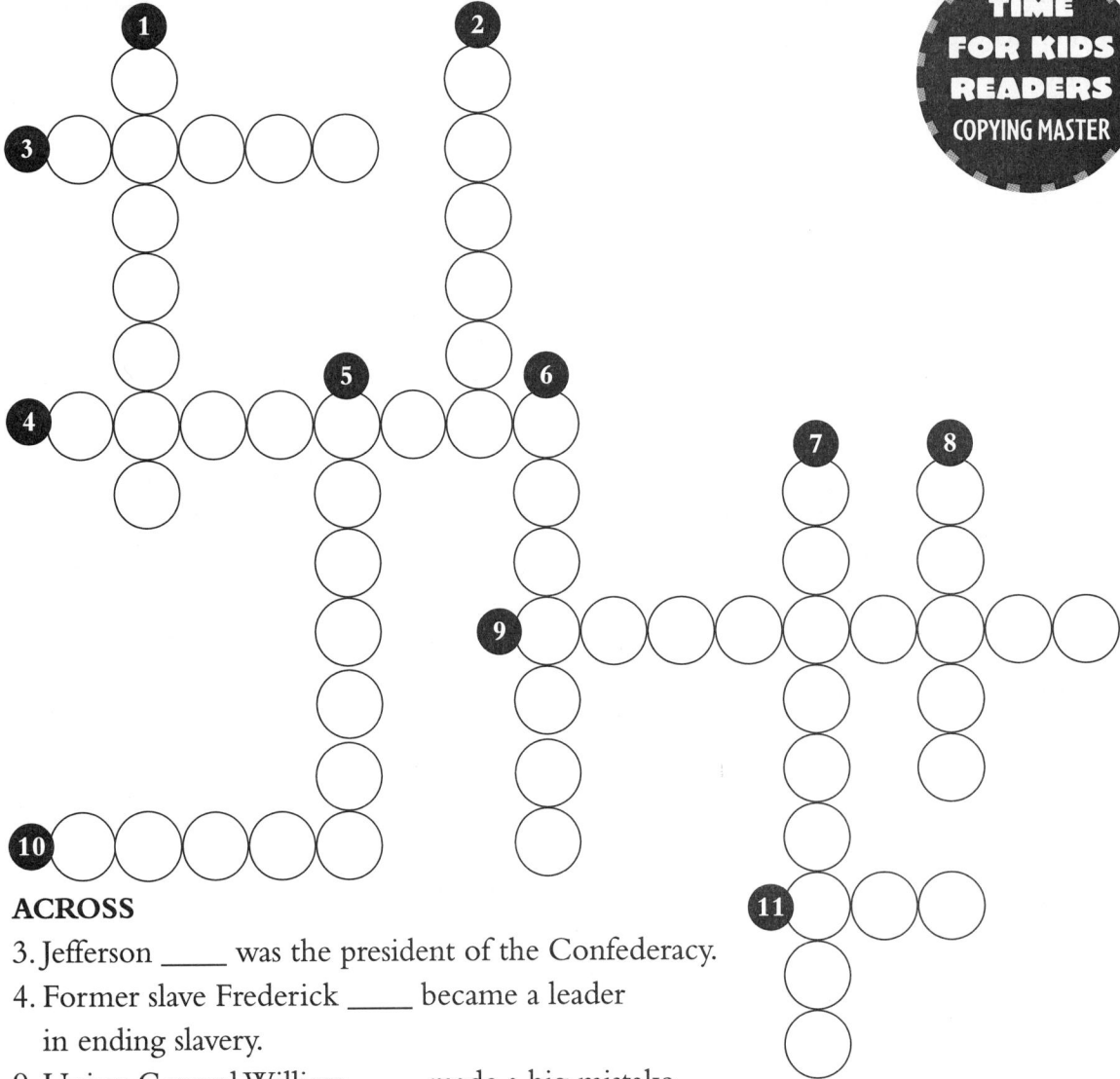

TIME
FOR KIDS
READERS
COPYING MASTER

ACROSS

3. Jefferson _____ was the president of the Confederacy.

4. Former slave Frederick _____ became a leader
   in ending slavery.

9. Union General William _____ made a big mistake
   during the battle of Chickamauga.

10. John ___ tried to capture weapons at a U.S. Army arsenal in Harpers Ferry.

11. Robert E. _____ was a Confederate general.

DOWN

1. Thomas _____ was also called "Stonewall."

2. Union General George _____ was known as the "Rock of Chickamauga."

5. The President of the United States during the Civil War was Abraham _____.

6. William _____ led the Union armies in Tennessee and Georgia.

7. George B. _____ helped keep the Confederate army out of the North.

8. Ulysses S. _____ was a Union general who was surprised at the battle of Shiloh.

© Harcourt

SITES OF THE CIVIL WAR

Home on the Plains

BACKGROUND

Summary

Although European explorers had traveled to the North American West as early as the late 1600s, very few Europeans settled in the Great Plains until the mid-1800s. As the eastern seaboard became more populated, however, more and more European Americans began to travel westward. Life on the plains was often challenging, but it provided these settlers with valuable land and new opportunities.

READING TIPS

Building Background

■ Write the word *pioneer* on the chalkboard. Challenge students to define or explain the word. (Possible response: someone who works in a new field or explores an unknown territory) Have students make the connection between this definition and the pioneers of the 1800s. Remind students that while North America's western regions were unknown to European settlers, they had been home to various Native American groups for thousands of years.

Reading for Details

■ Where are the Great Plains? (The Great Plains stretch from Canada to the Gulf of Mexico in central North America.)
■ Why was the Homestead Act of 1862 important? (It encouraged European settlers to move west by selling them 160 acres for $10.)
■ What does the word *prairie* mean in French? ("grazed meadow")
■ What is another term for a covered wagon? (a prairie schooner)
■ Who were the sodbusters? (people who built their homes out of sod)
■ Which important resource was scarce on the Great Plains? (water)
■ Where did people on the Great Plains go to buy their clothing? (They didn't. They fixed or sewed old clothing they had brought with them.)
■ Which natural forces caused many pioneers to leave the Great Plains? (tornadoes, drought)

Critical Thinking

■ Challenge students to think of words or short phrases that describe what life was like for the pioneers on the Great Plains. (Possible responses: difficult, challenging, exciting, new) Write the book's title on the chalkboard within a circle, and record students' descriptive words and phrases in surrounding circles to create a word web.
■ Ask students if they would have chosen to travel west in a covered wagon to make a new life on the Great Plains. Why or why not?

FAST FACTS

■ Native American people were the first inhabitants of the Great Plains. Groups such as the Sioux, Comanche, and Blackfoot Indians lived there for thousands of years. In the 1800s, however, the United States government forced many Native American people off their lands.

■ During the early part of United States history, two things kept many European settlers in the East: 1) the East Coast was closer to their "motherlands" in Europe; and 2) in order to travel west, one had to cross the Appalachian Mountain range, a difficult journey that few travelers wanted to face.

■ Before 1848, much of the land in the West did not belong to the United States. Through wars and treaties, the United States was eventually able to expand its territory all the way to the west coast.

■ In the late 1800s, the invention of the railroad supported the continued westward expansion of the United States.

Activity

■ **A Full Wagon:** When the pioneers decided to move, they could take with them only what would fit in a covered wagon or other small vehicle. Ask students to imagine that they are pioneers who are about to begin their journey to the Great Plains. Have students draw the outline of a covered wagon on a sheet of paper. Inside the wagon, have them list the items that they would take. On another sheet of paper, have students write a sentence or two to explain each item and why they chose to bring it along.

Vocabulary

covered wagon: a large, wooden wagon with a canvas cover spread over metal hoops

drought: a long spell of very dry weather

dugout: a home built into the side of a hill on the prairie

malaria: a serious disease that people get from the bite of an infected mosquito

pioneer: a person who explores unknown territory

prairie: a large area of flat or rolling grassland with few or no trees

seaboard: the land along or near an ocean shore

settler: a person who makes a home in a new place

sod: the top layer of soil and the grass attached to it

stagecoach: a coach, pulled by one or more horses, used in the past to carry passengers and mail over long
distances

wagon train: a line or group of covered wagons that traveled west together for safety

EXTENSION ACTIVITIES

LOOKING AT ILLUSTRATIONS

Curriculum Area: Social Studies

Skills: Observation, Critical Thinking

Have students study the illustration on pages 4–5 that shows a pioneer family camping beside their covered wagon. Ask: How large is the covered wagon? How many people are traveling in it? What is the family's clothing like? What do these details show about pioneer life?

THEN AND NOW

Curriculum Area: Social Studies

Skills: Recalling Facts, Note Taking, Organizing Information, Comparing and Contrasting

Distribute copies of page 39, which invites students to compare the lives of prairie children of the 1800s with the lives of children in the United States today. Review the sections on the chart: Food, Homes, and Activities. Have students work in pairs to find information in the book about each category. Finally, have students write brief essays based on the information contained in their charts. In what ways are their lives similar to the lives of prairie children of the 1800s? In what ways are they different?

ANSWER KEY

COPYING MASTERS

Page 39 Students should include at least two specific details in each section of the chart. Essays should be written in standard form, including an introduction, a paragraph about food, a paragraph about homes, a paragraph about activities, and a conclusion.

Page 40 1. s, **2.** o, **3.** d, **4.** d, **5.** i, **6.** e, **7.** s;
Final Word: soddies

READER

Think and Respond 1. corn; **2.** White settlers wanted to have their own land to live on and to cultivate. **3.** In 1862 the U.S. Congress passed the Homestead Act to encourage people to move to the western part of the country; people received 160 acres of land for $10 in return for promising to improve the land. **4.** Possible responses: drought, heat, cold winters, insects; **5.** Students should use examples from the reader to support their answers.

Write a Short Story Students' stories should accurately reflect the culture of the midwestern United States in the 1860s.

Name_____

Then and Now

Fill in the chart below. In the "Then" column, write about what life was like for pioneer children on the prairie in the 1800s. In the "Now" column, write about what life is like for you today.

	Then	**Now**
Food		
Homes		
Activities		

On a separate sheet of paper, write a brief essay based on the information in your chart. How is your life similar to the life of a prairie child of the 1800s? How is it different? Would you have liked to live on the prairie? Why or why not?

© Harcourt

Sodbusters

Answer each of the multiple-choice questions below. Then write the letter of each answer on the lines at the bottom of the page. If you answered the questions correctly, the letters will spell a word that was familiar to pioneers who built homes on the Great Plains.

1. What was a long line of covered wagons called?
(r) a wagon line
(s) a wagon train
(t) a chuck wagon
(u) a wagon wheel

2. What did pioneers often use for windows?
(m) glass
(n) linen with oil
(o) paper with bacon grease
(p) plastic

3. What were homes that were built into the sides of hills on the prairie called?
(a) hillies
(b) sideouts
(c) diggies
(d) dugouts

4. What are buffalo chips?
(c) potato chips
(d) animal droppings
(e) buffalo hides
(f) puzzle pieces

5. Which animal was dangerous because it destroyed crops?
(h) snakes
(i) grasshoppers
(j) buffalo
(k) deer

6. Which natural disaster occurred in the late 1800s that forced many people to leave the Great Plains?
(e) drought
(f) tornado
(g) flood
(h) snow

7. Which of these words does not describe people who tried to live on the prairie?
(p) ambitious
(q) resourceful
(r) hardworking
(s) lazy

Now write the letters of each answer on the lines below to answer this question: What did pioneers call houses made of sod?

____ ____ ____ ____ ____ ____ ____
   1   2   3   4   5   6   7

America's Other Coast: The Great Lakes

BACKGROUND

Summary

The word *beach* usually refers to a place where the land meets the ocean. Nevertheless, more than 10,000 miles (16,000 km) of beaches are located right in the middle of the North American continent. The Great Lakes are home to beautiful beaches, abundant wildlife, and more. The regions surrounding the lakes are rich in history, natural resources, industry, and recreation.

READING TIPS

Building Background

■ Ask students to describe a day at the beach. Create a word web with the word *beach* in the center. In surrounding circles, write the words and phrases that the students suggest. (Possible responses: waves, sand, blankets, people swimming, fish) Many students will associate beaches with ocean settings. Ask if they would consider the sandy shores of a lake a beach, too.

Reading for Details

■ What lies to the north of the Great Lakes? (the Canadian provinces of Ontario and Quebec)

■ What lies to the south of the Great Lakes? (the states of Minnesota, Michigan, Wisconsin, Illinois, Indiana, Pennsylvania, and New York)

■ Why is Lake Superior sometimes called "the most treacherous of the Great Lakes"? (It is very deep and very cold, and the weather can be stormy.)

■ How is Lake Michigan different from the other Great Lakes? (It is the only one that lies completely within the borders of the United States.)

■ If someone wanted to see some of the 180 species of fish that live in the Great Lakes, where could they go? (the Great Lakes Aquarium on the shore of Lake Superior)

■ If someone attended the Inland Seas Education Association, what would they learn about? (the plants and animals that exist in the Great Lakes region)

■ How did glaciers form the Great Lakes? (As sheets of ice, or glaciers, moved and melted, they carved out large chunks of land, leaving behind the basins of the Great Lakes.)

Critical Thinking

■ Life on the Great Lakes has changed dramatically since the arrival of European people. How has modernization affected the Great Lakes' environment? (Possible responses: More people live in the Great Lakes region; more businesses are located in the area; many trees have been cut down; there is more pollution; some species of plants and animals are threatened with extinction.)

FAST FACTS

■ The combined surface area of the five Great Lakes is 94,460 square miles (244,650 sq km).

■ Four of the lakes—Erie, Huron, Superior, and Ontario—form part of the border between the United States and Canada.

■ The Saint Lawrence River, which flows from Lake Ontario to the Gulf of Saint Lawrence in eastern Canada, is one of the main river outlets of the lake system.

■ Although Lake Erie is the smallest lake by volume, Lake Ontario (the smallest by surface area) is generally considered the smallest of the Great Lakes. The largest is Lake Superior.

■ The shores of the Great Lakes are home to four of the largest cities in North America: Chicago, Detroit, Toronto, and Cleveland.

■ Students can remember the names of the Great Lakes by recalling that the first letter of each name spells the word HOMES: Huron, Ontario, Michigan, Erie, Superior.

Vocabulary

dune: a sand hill made by the wind

ecosystem: a community of animals and plants interacting with their environment

glacier: a huge sheet of ice found in mountain valleys or polar regions

grassland: an area that is covered by grass or grasslike vegetation

hardwood: strong, hard wood from various trees, such as oak, beech, or ash

ice cap: a mound of ice that covers an area of land and expands outward as snow falls, melts, and freezes

logging: the cutting down of trees to sell the wood

resource: something valuable or useful

EXTENSION ACTIVITIES

LOOKING AT PHOTOGRAPHS

Curriculum Area: Social Studies

Skills: Observation, Critical Thinking

Divide the class into groups and ask each group to select a photograph from the book to study, using the following questions as a guide: What details do you notice about the picture's setting? How are people enjoying the lake? What does this photograph show about the Great Lakes region?

UNDERSTANDING GLACIERS

Curriculum Area: Science

Skills: Hands-on Experimentation, Recording Observations, Drawing Conclusions, Recognizing Cause and Effect, Making Connections

To help students understand how glaciers helped form the Great Lakes basin, divide the class into small groups, and give each group a plastic tub filled with sand. Tell students to pile the sand into a hill. Then give each group an ice cube to place on top of the hill. Allow students to check on their tubs every 10 minutes or so, each time drawing a picture of the hill and cube and writing a sentence to describe the changes that have taken place. Once the cube has melted, encourage students to draw conclusions about how the melting ice affected the hill of sand. Challenge them to make the connection between their experiment and the changes a glacier can cause over thousands of years of moving and melting over a land area.

WATER SCHOOL

Curriculum Areas: Social Studies, Language Arts, Art

Skills: Note Taking, Organizing Information, Visual Presentation, Group Work

Divide the students into groups of four and have them create informational posters about the Great Lakes. Distribute copies of page 43 and direct students to take notes from the book about each topic listed on the chart. Each group member will be responsible for creating a poster about one of these topics. Hang the finished posters in one of the school's public spaces to educate other students about the Great Lakes region.

ANSWER KEY

COPYING MASTERS

Page 43 Students should include at least three specific examples in each section of the chart. Students' posters should explain these examples and should include illustrations that clearly relate to that information.

Page 44 Students' poems should follow haiku form and should include specific details about the Great Lakes Region.

READER

Think and Respond 1. Superior, Huron, Erie, Michigan, Ontario; **2.** food, fresh water, water transportation, recreation, animal habitats; **3.** More than a million years ago, glaciers moved down slowly from the north; as they moved, they dug up Earth's surface and made deep and wide basins; eventually the ice melted, creating the Great Lakes. **4.** fishing, swimming, sailing, bird watching, canoeing; **5.** Students should give specific reasons for their choices.

Do Research Students' presentations should include information that was not included in the Reader. Encourage students to use visuals to support their research.

Great Lakes at a Glance

Fill in the chart below as you take notes about the Great Lakes.

Topic   **Notes**

Animals   _____

               _____

               _____

               _____

               _____

Plants   _____

               _____

               _____

               _____

               _____

Recreational
Activities   _____

               _____

               _____

               _____

Commercial
Activities   _____

               _____

               _____

               _____

               _____

Poetry of the Lakes

Haiku is a form of Japanese poetry that often uses nature as its theme. Read the following haiku about the Great Lakes region.

Lakes of mystery
Oceans surrounded by land
Full of life and lore

Now write a haiku poem of your own. Traditional haiku poems contain three lines with a total of seventeen syllables, divided like this:

Line 1: five syllables
Line 2: seven syllables
Line 3: five syllables

When people write haiku in languages other than Japanese, they don't always follow these exact syllable counts. But they do follow the basic form of three short lines, with the middle line slightly longer than the other two.

Write a first draft of your haiku in the space below:

Line 1:..

Line 2:...

Line 3:..

Trade your haiku with a partner. Give each other suggestions about how to improve your poems. Then copy your poem onto a sheet of plain white paper. Make a simple black-and-white drawing to illustrate your poem. Use the space below to make a sketch for your illustration.

Ohio State Fair

BACKGROUND

Summary

Every year in August, almost 1 million people gather in Columbus, Ohio, for the Ohio State Fair, an event that has been held for more than 150 years. Originally designed to celebrate the state's agricultural products, the fair now includes rides, contests, and a variety of shows and entertainment, as well as the agricultural displays that made it famous throughout the state so long ago.

READING TIPS

Building Background

■ Have any students been to the Ohio State Fair? What was it like?

■ Tell students that Ohio's first State Fair took place more than 150 years ago. How do they think fairs have changed since then? (See background summary.)

Reading for Details

■ What was the original purpose of the Ohio State Fair? (It was an agricultural exposition.)

FAST FACTS

■ The Ohio State Fair is held at the Ohio Expo Center in Columbus, Ohio.

■ Exhibits are held both indoors and outdoors.

■ Vendors who wish to sell products or concessions during the fair pay a fee to rent retail space.

■ The fair includes a junior fair, livestock competitions, a horse show, arts-and-crafts exhibits, and horticulture and floriculture competitions.

■ The fair also has a Memory Wall, where fairgoers can share their memories of past fairs.

■ In what year did the first Ohio State Fair take place? (1850)

■ How long does the present Ohio State Fair last? (17 days)

■ Where is the Ohio State Fair held now? (the Ohio Expo Center)

■ If you wanted to go on the rides at the fair, which part of the fairgrounds would you visit? (the Midway)

■ What was one of the first forms of entertainment offered for children at the fair? (pony rides)

■ If you were hungry, how many food vendors would you have to choose from? (175)

■ Why might attendance at the fair have gone down from 2000 to 2001? (Weather often determines how many people attend the fair; rainy or very hot weather keeps people away.)

■ What advice does Cathi Baumgardner offer fairgoers? (She advises fairgoers to wear comfortable shoes.)

Critical Thinking

■ Why do you think state fairs began? (Originally fairs were held as a way to sell farm produce and animals. Farm people tended to live isolated lives, so when they came into town, they enjoyed having a good time.)

■ Have students consider what is special about their state or region. If your community hosted a local fair, what products might it feature? What kinds of competitions might it include?

Activity

■ **Come One, Come All:** Challenge students to design an advertising campaign to attract visitors to the Ohio State Fair. Divide the class into groups and invite them to brainstorm ideas. Which aspects of the fair will they highlight in their campaigns? Encourage students to think of a catchy slogan for the fair and to include this slogan in posters, flyers, television ads, radio spots, billboards, or bumper stickers.

Vocabulary

attendance: the number of people present at an event

bird's-eye view: a view seen from high above

cholera: a dangerous disease that causes severe illness and diarrhea

dormitory: a building with many separate sleeping rooms

exhibitors: people who show things to the public

exposition: a public exhibition

livestock: animals raised on a farm or ranch, such as horses, sheep, and cows

EXTENSION ACTIVITIES

WHAT I SAW AT THE FAIR

Curriculum Area: Language Arts
Skills: Imagination, Letter-Writing

Have students look at the pictures on pages 10–13, which show visitors enjoying themselves at the Ohio State Fair. Then ask students to imagine that they have just come home from a wonderful day at the fair. Have them write letters to friends or relatives describing their experiences. What did they do? What did they see? What sounds did they hear? What scents did they smell? What foods did they taste? Did they win any prizes? Which rides did they like the best? How do they feel about their experiences?

FAIR OF THE FUTURE

Curriculum Area: Social Studies
Skills: Critical Thinking, Comparing and Contrasting

After students have completed the activity on page 47, have them work in pairs to imagine what the Ohio State Fair might be like 150 years from now. Where will the fair be held? What will the cost of admission be? How many people will attend? How will they get there? What special exhibitions, competitions, or forms of entertainment will the Fair of the Future include?

FUN AT THE MIDWAY

Curriculum Areas: Language Arts, Art
Skills: Imagination, Planning, Presentation, Group Work

The midway at a fair features carnival rides and booths where people can win prizes such as stuffed animals for games such as tossing a nickel in an empty goldfish bowl. Divide the class into groups, and challenge students to create their own games of challenge and chance. If possible, allow students to set up tables in the school gym or cafeteria and give them an hour or two to try out each other's games. Encourage them to decorate their booths and to take turns as "barkers" urging their classmates to try the game.

ANSWER KEY

COPYING MASTERS

Page 47

Site: Then—Cincinnati, 8–10 acres, sometimes moved to different towns; Now— Ohio Expo Center in Columbus, 360 acres

Admission: Then—20 cents; Now—8 dollars

Attendance: Then—25,000 to 30,000 people; Now—nearly a million people

Transportation: Then—by horse or train; Now—by car, tour bus, or recreational vehicle

Things to See and Do: Then—agricultural exhibits, pony rides, dancing monkeys; Now—agricultural exhibits, amusement rides, concerts by popular entertainers, competitions

Page 48 Students' poems should follow the suggested format and should include a wide variety of sensory details.

READER

Think and Respond 1. 4-H is an organization where young people learn new skills, build self-confidence, learn responsibility, and achieve goals. **2.** It was an agricultural fair for farmers to show off their best crops and farm animals. **3.** view livestock and agricultural crops; enjoy amusement rides, food vendors, and performances; **4.** Possible responses: sporting events, weddings, social clubs

Write About an Exhibit Encourage students to select objects that have personal or cultural significance for them.

OHIO STATE FAIR

Name_____

The Ohio State Fair—
Then and Now

A lot can happen in a century and a half! Fill in the chart below to show how the Ohio State Fair has changed since it first began 150 years ago.

	Then	Now
Site		
Admission		
Attendance		
Transportation		
Things to See and Do		

Now organize your ideas into an essay with the title "The Ohio State Fair—Then and Now." Be sure that your essay includes an introduction, a body, and a conclusion.

Fairground Poetry

Write a poem that captures the experience of a day at the Ohio State Fair. Each line should start with one of the letters in the words *State Fair.* Include lots of details, such as sights you can see, sounds you can hear, scents you can smell, foods you can taste, things you can touch, activities you can do, and feelings you can have at the State Fair.

TIME FOR KIDS READERS
COPYING MASTER

S_____

T_____

A_____

T_____

E_____

F_____

A_____

I _____

R_____

Bonus: Copy your poem onto a large sheet of paper, and include a small illustration for each line.

Look Out for Lava

BACKGROUND

Summary

Over the centuries, volcanoes have brought danger and destruction to people around the world. So why would anyone want to work around volcanoes every day? To learn about them, of course! As a volcanologist in Hawaii, Christina Heliker studies the reasons volcanoes behave as they do. From unexpected eruptions to constant lava flows, learning about and exploring volcanic activity is all in a day's work.

READING TIPS

Building Background

■ Discuss what students have read, heard, or seen about volcanoes. What kinds of damage can they cause? What dangers do volcanoes pose to people who live near them? How do students think scientists study volcanoes? Invite volunteers to come to the board to draw what a volcano looks like.

FAST FACTS

■ Volcanoes exist on every continent. Many volcanoes are located along the edges of the earth's plates, which are large chunks of the earth's crust that shift and move.

■ Although new volcanoes sometimes form, scientists estimate that most volcanoes have been around for millions of years.

■ Scientists believe that volcanoes not only helped form the earth's surface but also contributed to the atmosphere.

■ The Hawaiian Islands were formed by volcanoes that erupted underwater millions of years ago.

■ Scientists believe that about 500 of the world's volcanoes are active. Of those 500, about 20 to 30 may erupt each year.

■ A volcano that has not erupted in many years is called dormant, or sleeping.

Reading for Details

■ What is the word for a scientist who studies volcanoes? (volcanologist)

■ What do the letters HVO stand for? (Hawaiian Volcano Observatory)

■ How is Christina Heliker able to walk on a volcano? (She wears clothing that won't burn, leather gloves, and heavy boots. Sometimes she wears a gas mask.)

■ How many people have died because of erupting volcanoes in the past 500 years? (300,000)

■ How is Mount St. Helens different from the volcanoes of Hawaii? (Mount St. Helens is a composite volcano, which can explode violently. The volcanoes of Hawaii are shield volcanoes, which erupt more gently.)

■ Why is being able to fly above a volcano helpful to a volcanologist? (It allows a volcanologist to map new lava flows, take photographs of changing conditions, and get a different perspective on the volcano.)

■ What do lava samples help scientists predict? (how much longer an eruption could last)

■ How can predictions about volcanic activity be helpful? (Predictions about volcanic activity can help save lives.)

Critical Thinking

■ Ask students to think of words that describe the job of a volcanologist. (Possible responses: exciting, challenging, scary) What kind of person might decide to become a volcanologist? (Possible responses: someone with an interest in science, someone who is brave and adventurous, someone who enjoys traveling to new places)

Activity

Location, Location, Location: Review the names of the volcanoes mentioned in the book (Kilauea, Mauna Loa, Mount St. Helens, Mount

Pinatubo). Divide the class into groups, and challenge each group to find the geographical location of each volcano, referring to encyclopedias, almanacs, atlases, and Web sites. When students have completed their research, review the volcanoes' locations as a class. Say the name of a volcano, and invite a student volunteer to show the class its location on a classroom map.

Vocabulary

composite volcano: a volcano that explodes violently

crater: the mouth of a volcano or geyser

eruption: an event in which a volcano throws up rocks, hot ashes, and lava with great force

flow: something that moves along smoothly like a river

geologist: a person who studies the earth's layers of soil and rock

hectare: a unit of area in the metric system; one hectare is equal to 10,000 square meters

landslide: a sudden slide of earth and rocks down the side of a mountain or a hill

lava: the hot, liquid rock that pours out of a volcano when it erupts

magma: melted rock found beneath the earth's surface that flows as lava out of active volcanoes

mudflow: earth that is wet, soft, sticky, and moving like a river

observatory: a building containing telescopes and other scientific equipment for studying something up close, usually the sky and the stars

outburst: a sudden pouring out

pyroclastic flow: a fast-moving cloud of hot gases and pieces of rock

shield volcano: a volcano that erupts gently

volcanologist: a scientist who studies volcanoes

EXTENSION ACTIVITIES

LOOKING AT PHOTOGRAPHS

Curriculum Area: Social Studies

Skills: Observation, Critical Thinking

Have students use the following questions as a guide to discuss the photographs on pages 8–9 of the book that show Christina Heliker working near a volcano: Where is Christina Heliker? (at the site of a recent volcanic eruption) What is she doing?

(collecting lava samples) How would you describe her job? (Possible responses: exciting, challenging)

VOLCANO VISITORS

Curriculum Areas: Science, Language Arts

Skills: Critical Thinking, Research, Presentation, Group Work

Have students work in groups to set up a "Visitors, Center" at the Hawaiian Volcano Observatory. As a class, brainstorm different types of objects and information that such a center might include (for example, examples of the clothing that volcanologists wear; pictures of instruments they use; a diagram that explains how volcanoes erupt; a time line that shows important volcanic eruptions throughout history; a map of major volcano locations throughout the world). Make each group responsible for presenting one type of information. Then combine all the groups' end products to create your classroom Visitors, Center.

ANSWER KEY

COPYING MASTERS

Page 51 After identifying volcanoes to study, students may refer to the book as well as other resources for specific information.

Page 52 **1.** volcano, **2.** Helens, **3.** crust, **4.** eruption, **5.** lava, **6.** Hilo, **7.** Pinatubo, **8.** flows; **Final word:** Vesuvius

READER

Think and Respond **1.** Kilauea, Mauna Loa; **2.** by collecting rock and lava samples; by flying over the volcano in a helicopter; by using seismometers that measure the shaking of the Earth; **3.** a type of mountain that releases lava, rock, ash, and gas; **4.** 1,500; **5.** Possible responses: Yes, it would be good to study volcanoes and to help people; no, it is too dangerous.

Write a Report Students' reports should include volcano locations and descriptions of the volcanoes' history, development, and distinctive features.

Name_____

Out in the Field

Imagine you are a volcanologist observing a volcano. Choose an actual volcano to study. Then write about your day in the field by researching answers to the questions below.

Date:	Volcano:

Location:

What do you observe about the lava?

▶ _____
_____
_____
_____

What do you observe about the ground?

▶ _____
_____
_____
_____

What do you observe about the air?

▶ _____
_____
_____
_____

What conclusions can you draw based on your observations? What predictions can you make about this volcano?

_____
_____
_____
_____
_____

Name _____

A Famous Volcano

Complete each sentence with the correct word. Then write the
circled letters in order on the lines below to form the name of
a volcano that erupted 2,000 years ago.

1. A ◯ ___ ___ ___ ___ ___ ___ is a hole in the earth's
surface.

2. Mount St. ___ ◯ ___ ___ ___ ___ is a volcano that erupted in
Washington state.

3. The ___ ___ ___ ◯ ___ is the top layer of the earth.

4. When a volcano explodes, it is called an ___ ___ ◯ ___ ___ ___ ___ ___.

5. ___ ___ ◯ ___ is hot melted rock that flows from a volcano.

6. The Hawaii town of ___ ◯ ___ ___ is in the path of lava flows from
two volcanoes.

7. Mount ___ ___ ___ ___ ___ ◯ ___ ___ is a volcano in the
Philippines.

8. Rivers of lava are also called ___ ___ ___ ___ ◯.

Which volcano erupted in Italy in A.D. 79?

Mount ___ ___ ___ ___ ___ ___ ___ ___

Volcano Fact: Many valuable gems and minerals form as a result of volcanic
activity. Here are a few: • aquamarines • copper • diamonds • gold
• moonstones • opals • silver • topaz

© Harcourt

TIME FOR KIDS READERS
Angel Island

BACKGROUND

Summary

During the first half of the twentieth century, many immigrants came to California from Asia. Before they were allowed to enter the United States, they had to pass through the immigration center at Angel Island. The experiences of Asian Americans at Angel Island illustrate the dreams that have brought millions of immigrants to the United States, as well as the challenges that many of them have faced along the way.

READING TIPS

Building Background

■ Write the word *immigrant* on the chalkboard, and ask students to explain what it means. (Possible response: someone who leaves his or her native country to live in a new country) Ask students to list some of the countries from which immigrants to the United States have come.

FAST FACTS

■ Angel Island is the largest island in San Francisco Bay, which lies between the cities of San Francisco and Oakland.

■ The Spanish first explored the island in 1775.

■ From 1863 to 1946 the United States used the island as an army base.

■ During World War II, the U.S. Army held prisoners of war on Angel Island.

■ Between 1910 and 1940, approximately 230,000 Asian immigrants passed through Angel Island. That's about 7,667 people per year, or about 21 people per day.

■ Today Angel Island is a state park, where people can hike, camp, bicycle, and sunbathe.

■ Did any students or their parents immigrate to the United States? If so, invite students and parents to share personal experiences with the rest of the class.

Reading for Details

■ How are Ellis Island and Angel Island alike? (Both places were stations for processing and admitting immigrants to the United States.)

■ How are Ellis Island and Angel Island different? (Ellis Island is on the East Coast and mostly processed people from Europe. Angel Island is on the West Coast and mostly processed people from Asia.)

■ In what year did Albert Wong arrive in the United States? (1934)

■ When did immigrants from China first begin to arrive in the United States? Why did they come? (They arrived in San Francisco during the gold rush years, many with the hope of finding gold.)

■ How is the Chinese Exclusion Act of 1882 different from any other law ever passed in the United States? (It is the only law that prevented a particular group of people from entering the country.)

■ Why might some immigrants on Angel Island have been tempted to swim across the water to U.S. soil? (Many immigrants feared that they would not be allowed to enter the United States. If they were able to escape the island and swim to San Francisco, they would not have to go through the immigration process.)

Critical Thinking

■ Ask students what character traits the Asian immigrants must have had in order to face their challenges at Angel Island. (Possible responses: patience, bravery, determination, hope) Do students think they could endure the same experiences if they were in this situation?

Activity

■ **Dear Dad:** Remind students that because Albert Wong and his father were not able to stay in the same building on Angel Island, they had to communicate through letters. Divide the class into pairs and have each pair write a series of letters between Albert and his father. One partner will be Albert while the other will be his father. Suggest that "Albert" write first to describe his day and how he felt about it. Upon reading the letter, "Dad" will respond, writing about his own experiences and feelings. Encourage students to write at least two letters each, reflecting the content of the book.

Vocabulary

barracks: the building or buildings in which soldiers live

character: a letter, figure, or other mark used in printing

citizen: a member of a particular country who has the right to live there

ferry: a boat or ship that regularly carries people across a stretch of water

immigrant: a person who comes from one country to live permanently in another country

steerage: the section of a passenger ship that costs the least to travel in

wilderness: an area of wild land where no people live, such as a dense forest

EXTENSION ACTIVITIES

LOOKING AT PHOTOGRAPHS

Curriculum Area: Social Studies
Skills: Observation, Critical Thinking

Have students look at the photograph on page 13 of the book. Ask: What is happening in the photograph? (Asian immigrants are having their papers checked by immigration officials.) How would you feel if you were one of the immigrants pictured in this photograph? (Possible responses: excited, nervous, hopeful)

ISLAND POETRY

Curriculum Area: Language Arts
Skill: Creative Writing

Invite a volunteer to read the poem presented in the book. Remind students that many Chinese immi-grants wrote poems during their stay on Angel Island. Talk with students about how this poem reflects their experiences. Then discuss the poetic style of the poem, pointing out that it doesn't rhyme, it is not very long, and it doesn't have a specific rhythm. Encourage students to write other short, freestyle poems that reflect the immigrant experience at Angel Island. Suggest that students think about how Albert Wong felt and the things he did while detained there. If he had written a poem, what might he have said?

STARTING A BUSINESS

Curriculum Area: Social Studies
Skills: Critical Thinking, Problem Solving

Recall with students that Albert's grandfather started his own business when he arrived in the United States. Ask students what kind of business they might like to start if they moved to a new place. Encourage them to consider what needs their business could address and how it could benefit their community. Invite students to share their business ideas. How many students started restaurants? Clothing stores? Services? Entertainment venues? Tally up their choices. Which types of businesses are most popular? Why?

ANSWER KEY

COPYING MASTERS

Page 55 **1.** e, **2.** a, **3.** g, **4.** d, **5.** c, **6.** f, **7.** b

Page 56 **1.** 7,667 per year; **2.** 21 per day; **3.** 193,548 per year; **4.** 530 per day; **5.** 11,770,000 more; **6.** 509 more; **7.** 13,333

READER

Think and Respond **1.** Angel Island is near San Fran-cisco; Ellis Island is near New York City. **2.** to accommodate the many immigrants who came from Asian countries; **3.** China, Japan, Korea, the Philippines, Australia, Africa, Russia; **4.** Angel Island: 230,000; Ellis Island: 12,000,000; **5.** Writing poetry was a way for immigrants to make sense of a difficult experience; it was also a way to share their stories with others.

Write a Poem Students' poems should express their feelings about a significant event.

Chain Reaction

The following events led up to the creation of the immigration center at Angel Island, but they are out of order. Work with your group to put the statements in the correct sequence. Use the book to find the information you need.

_____ a. After the gold rush ended, many Asian immigrants remained in the country to begin their own businesses.

_____ b. Asian immigrants had to go through a rigorous immigration process at Angel Island that involved weeks of interviews and background checks.

_____ c. Some United States residents began to resent immigrant workers, particularly those of non-European backgrounds.

_____ d. The railroad was completed, and many people were unemployed.

_____ e. The first Asian immigrants, mostly Chinese men, arrived during the gold rush.

_____ f. The United States enacted the Chinese Exclusion Act of 1882.

_____ g. Many Chinese men assisted in the construction of the Transcontinental Railroad.

Think About It:

Did things have to happen this way? Why or why not? What if one of these events hadn't happened? How might things have turned out differently? Begin your answer on the lines below, and finish on another sheet of paper.

_____

_____

_____

_____

_____

Immigration Statistics

Answer the questions below in the space provided. Show your work on the right-hand side of the page.

1. From 1910 to 1940, Angel Island processed about 230,000 Asian immigrants. On average, how many Asian immigrants did Angel Island process each year over this 30-year span?

_____

2. On average how many Asian immigrants did Angel Island process each day?

_____

3. From 1892 to 1954, Ellis Island processed about 12,000,000 immigrants. On average, how many immigrants did Ellis Island process each year over this 62-year span?

_____

4. On average how many immigrants did Ellis Island process each day?

_____

5. How many more immigrants did Ellis Island process on average over its history than the Asian immigrants processed at Angel Island?

_____

6. How many more immigrants did Ellis Island process on average each day compared with the number of Asian immigrants processed on average each day at Angel Island?

_____

7. Between 1867 and 1870, approximately 40,000 Chinese immigrants arrived in the United States. On average, how many immigrants arrived each year over this three-year span?

_____

The Pony Express

BACKGROUND

Summary

In the United States today, the U.S. Postal Service delivers the mail almost every day through an organized system overseen by the U.S. government. In the mid-1800s, the United States had no mail system like this. It could take up to three weeks for mail to travel from one end of the country to the other. The Pony Express sought to solve this problem by delivering mail more quickly to the West Coast.

READING TIPS

Building Background

■ Talk with students about modern communication, including various features of today's mail system (for example, mail carriers, post offices, stamps, express and overnight services). Invite students to talk about the use of e-mail, telephones, television, and radio to relay news and information. How do they think people communicated across long distances 140 years ago?

Reading for Details

■ What happened in St. Joseph, Missouri, on April 3, 1860? (The Pony Express began operating on this day from this town.)

■ How long did it take the Pony Express to deliver mail from Missouri to California? (10½ days)

■ How did Johnny Frey cross the Missouri River? (He and his horse traveled across the river on a ferry.)

■ What happened five days after the first Pony Express rider left Missouri? (The westbound rider, who had departed from Missouri, met the eastbound rider, who had departed from Sacramento.)

■ Why did some people feel the Pony Express would not be successful? (Traveling across the country was difficult at that time. Not many settlements existed, and riders faced many dangers.)

■ What two things contributed to the demise of the Pony Express? (The invention of the telegraph meant people could send messages faster. Also, the company that had started the Pony Express had financial difficulties.)

Critical Thinking

■ Discuss the dangers and excitement that Pony Express riders might have faced. What might it have been like to ride through the Rocky Mountains? To cross the Great Plains? To encounter wild animals? Ask students if they would have wanted to be riders on the Pony Express. Why or why not?

Activity

■ **You've Got Mail:** Have students compare the way in which the mail was delivered 140 years ago with the way it is delivered today. (Possible responses: In the 1860s, the speediest way to deliver mail was by horse; today, the speediest way to communicate is by

FAST FACTS

■ The Pony Express lasted for only a year and a half—from April 1860 to October 1861.

■ The major stations at each end of the Pony Express were St. Joseph, Missouri, and Sacramento, California.

■ Most of the Pony Express riders were young men, many of them teenagers.

■ Riders were expected to travel about 75 miles (121 km) a day. Riders changed horses every 10 to 15 miles (16 to 24 km).

■ At its height, the Pony Express employed about 80 riders, stopped at more than 100 stations, and used between 400 and 500 horses.

fax or e-mail. Back then, delivery people were mostly teenage boys; today, they are adult men and women. Pony Express riders stopped at stations; today's mail carriers stop at post offices.)

Vocabulary

applicant: someone who has written formally asking for something, such as a job

bandit: an armed robber

ferry: a boat or ship that regularly carries people across a stretch of water

mochila: a mailbag

route: a predictable path traveled regularly by a person

settlement: a small village or group of houses

settler: a person who makes a home in a new place

stagecoach: a coach, pulled by one or more horses, used in the past to carry passengers and mail over long distances

wilderness: an area of wild land where no people live, such as a dense forest

EXTENSION ACTIVITIES

HELP WANTED

Curriculum Areas: Social Studies, Language Arts, Art
Skills: Reading For Details, Note Taking, Graphic Design
Remind students that the Pony Express company had specific qualifications for its riders. Ask students to look through the book and take notes about these qualifications. Then challenge students to turn those qualifications into a help-wanted ad. After students have written their ads, have them transfer them to posters so they can share them with classmates.

YOU'RE FAMOUS!

Curriculum Areas: Social Studies, Language Arts
Skills: Dramatization, Expository Writing
Recall with students that delivering the mail in 10½ days was big news in 1860. What do they imagine newspaper reporters might have asked those riders who arrived in Sacramento and St. Joseph? Divide the class into pairs, and ask each pair to create a dialogue between a reporter and a Pony Express rider. To extend the activity, have students rewrite their interviews as newspaper articles. Remind students that the first paragraph of a newspaper story tells *who, what, where, when, how,* and *why.* Have

students transfer their stories onto large sheets of newsprint to resemble the pages of a newspaper.

PONY EXPRESS POSTCARDS

Curriculum Areas: Social Studies, Language Arts, Art
Skills: Understanding Historical Perspective, Creative Writing
Distribute copies of page 59, which invites students to create commemorative stamps related to the Pony Express. After students have completed their sketches, have them create full-color versions of their stamps on sheets of 8½" x 11" paper. Students can trim the edges of the paper to resemble the edges of an actual stamp. Then hand out pieces of posterboard, which students will use to create larger-than-life postcards. Have each student attach his or her stamp to the postcard and then write a message expressing the experiences, thoughts, and feelings of a young rider on the Pony Express.

ANSWER KEY

COPYING MASTERS

Page 59 Students' designs should reflect significant people, events, or ideas associated with the Pony Express.

Page 60 1. true, **2.** true, **3.** false, **4.** false, **5.** true, **6.** false, **7.** false; **Final Answer:** Russell

READER

Think and Respond 1. the telegraph; **2.** People could receive news from both sides of the continent in a matter of days instead of months; express riders were able to exchange news and events as they passed in either direction. **3.** Riders had to be young, tough, fearless riders who weighed under 120 pounds. **4.** Possible responses: Mail can now be sorted and routed electronically; mail can be shipped overnight for delivery the next day; people can send e-mail over the Internet. **5.** Students should support their opinions with specific reasons.

Make a Graph Students' charts should include the mail's place and date of origin, its date of arrival, and the length of time it took the mail to be delivered.

Name_____

Pony Express Postage

Important parts of United States history are often commemorated on postage stamps. Design a stamp that recalls an important person, event, or idea associated with the Pony Express. Draw a sketch for your commemorative stamp in the space provided.

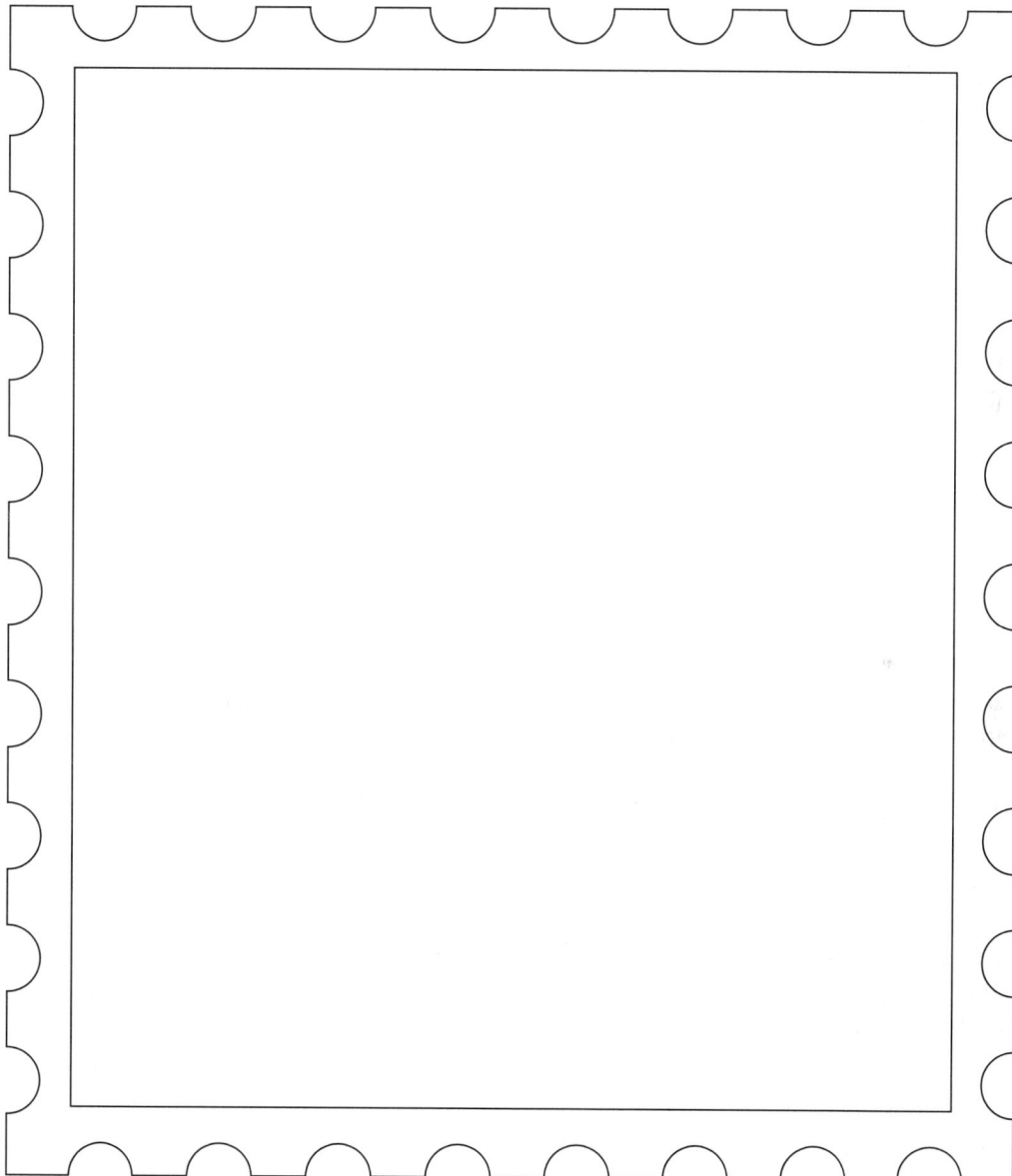

How Much Did It Cost?

A letter that weighed ½ ounce cost $5 to send via the Pony Express. That was quite a lot of money, compared to how much people earned in those days. If a rider made $25 a week and worked 5 days, it would cost him a day's salary to mail one letter! The price was later dropped to $1 for a ½-ounce letter.

© Harcourt

THE PONY EXPRESS

Pony Express— True or False?

Read the statements below. Decide if they are true or false. Write *true* or *false* on the lines. (If the answer is *true*, you will have one blank space left over.) Then follow the directions to reveal the name of a mystery person.

1. The Pony Express route was 2,000 miles long.

   ___ ⃝ ___ ___ ___ ___

2. The Pony Express began in 1860.

   ___ ___ ⃝ ___ ___ ___ ___

3. One rider traveled the entire length of the Pony Express route.

   ___ ___ ___ ⃝ ___ ___

4. The rider of the last Pony Express run was Buffalo Bill Cody.

   ___ ___ ___ ⃝ ___ ___

5. Riders took a ferry across the Missouri River.

   ___ ___ ___ ⃝ ___ ___

6. The Pony Express was so successful that even the invention of the telegraph could not stop it.

   ___ ___ ⃝ ___ ___ ___

7. One end of the Pony Express was St. Louis, Missouri. The other end was San Francisco, California.

   ___ ___ ⃝ ___ ___ ___

Now write the circled letters in order on the lines below to reveal the name of the mystery person.

The creator of the Pony Express was

William H. ____ ____ ____ ____ ____ ____ ____ .

Census 2000: Who We Are

BACKGROUND

Summary

Every ten years, the United States government conducts a census—an official count of all the people who live in the United States. It's not easy to track everyone down, especially with a population of more than 280 million people. It's important for people to fill out and return their census forms or agree to speak with an enumerator so the government can get important information it needs. The information obtained by the census provides a vital picture of who we, the people of the United States, are.

READING TIPS

Building Background

■ What is a census? (an official population count that includes information about characteristics such as age, gender, and occupation)

■ Why does the U.S. government need to know how many people live here? (Possible response:

FAST FACTS

■ A census is taken during the years that end with a zero (for example, 1980, 1990, 2000).

■ According to the latest census, about 275 million more people live in the United States than did when the first census was conducted in 1790.

■ The government first instituted the census in 1790 to determine how many congressional representatives each state should have.

■ States have 1 representative for every 600,000 people.

■ The census is more than just a count. It tallies ages, racial backgrounds, and other important statistics.

The government makes decisions about how to allocate resources based on how many people live in each state.)

Reading for Details

■ How has the way in which the census is conducted changed since 1790? (In 1790 the census was conducted by U.S. marshals on horseback. Today the census is conducted largely through the mail.)

■ In 1790, where did most people live? (on farms)

■ Today, where do most people in the United States *not* live? (on farms)

■ According to the 2000 census, what is the population of the United States? (281.4 million people)

■ How many people in the United States today are immigrants? (28.4 million people, or about 1 in every 10 residents)

■ Which cultural group has grown the most since the 1990 census? (Hispanic Americans)

■ What does *multiracial* mean? ("belonging to more than one race")

■ What is happening to houses in the United States? (They are getting bigger.)

Critical Thinking

■ Compare the results of the 1990 census with the results of the 2000 census. What major changes took place? (Possible responses: The U.S. population has grown; the average age of Americans has increased; there are more immigrants in the United States; there are more multiracial families.) What kinds of changes might we see when the next census takes place in 2010? (Possible response: The U.S. population will continue to grow and to become more diverse.)

Activity

■ **Class Census:** Have students conduct a "census" of the class. Assign students to pairs and tell each pair to think of a type of a question they could ask their classmates. Encourage students to stick to topics that are not too personal, such as birthday, eye color, or number of siblings. After all the pairs have decided on their questions, have them act as "enumerators" by polling their classmates in person to gather responses. Invite pairs to share their data with the class.

Vocabulary

census: an official count of all the people living in a country or district

data: information or facts

diversity: variety

ethnic: sharing the same national origins, language, or culture

immigrant: a person who comes from one country to live permanently in another country

marshal: an officer of a federal court who has duties similar to those of a sheriff

multiracial: involving people of different races; belonging to more than one race

official: someone who holds an important position in an organization, as in a government

representative: someone who is chosen to speak or act for others

EXTENSION ACTIVITIES

BROADCAST NEWS

Curriculum Areas: Social Studies, Language Arts
Skills: Applying Knowledge, Oral Presentation, Group Work
When the U.S. Census 2000 report first came out, news broadcasters reported the findings on television. Invite your students to create their own television news reports about the census. Divide the class into groups of five students each, and have the group members play the following roles: two news anchors who introduce the story; a reporter who joins the anchors to describe the census results while the anchors ask questions and make comments; a beat reporter out on the street interviewing passersby; and a person on the street whom the beat reporter asks to comment on the census results. If possible, videotape students' news broadcasts so they can later watch them on TV.

WE ARE YOUR FOURTH GRADE CLASS

Curriculum Areas: Social Studies, Language Arts
Skills: Group Participation, Organizing Information, Summarizing
On large sheets of chart paper, have students work in groups to create word webs that represent their own interests and activities. Initial categories might include Sports We Play, Pets We Have, Hobbies We Enjoy, Music We Like, and Our Favorite Foods. Encourage students to add other categories to the web and keep branching out from those. Then have each student write a brief paragraph summarizing one section of the web.

ANSWER KEY

COPYING MASTERS

Page 63 Part A: 1. White; Most U.S. residents are white; **2.** Hispanic or Latino and African American; their bars are almost the same length. **3.** 1%; **4.** Asian; **Part B:** Students' graphs should reflect the data.

Page 64 1. s, **2.** p, **3.** a, **4.** n, **5.** i, **6.** s, **7.** h; **Final Answer:** Spanish

READER

Think and Respond **1.** age, number of people in family, gender, ethnicity, occupation, income, and size and type of home; **2.** to understand population changes so the government can better meet people's needs; **3.** Nevada, Arizona, Colorado, Utah, and Idaho; **4.** In 1790, U.S. marshals rode by horseback from home to home; today, forms are sent by mail and enumerators follow up with home visits if necessary. **5.** Possible responses: tell them that if the government doesn't receive accurate information about their region, they might not get the money needed to support their schools or have the right number of seats in the House of Representatives; assure them that all the information on the form is confidential

Do Research Students should organize their data clearly and draw accurate comparisons between past and present.

Name_____

U.S. Census 2000 Graphing the U.S.

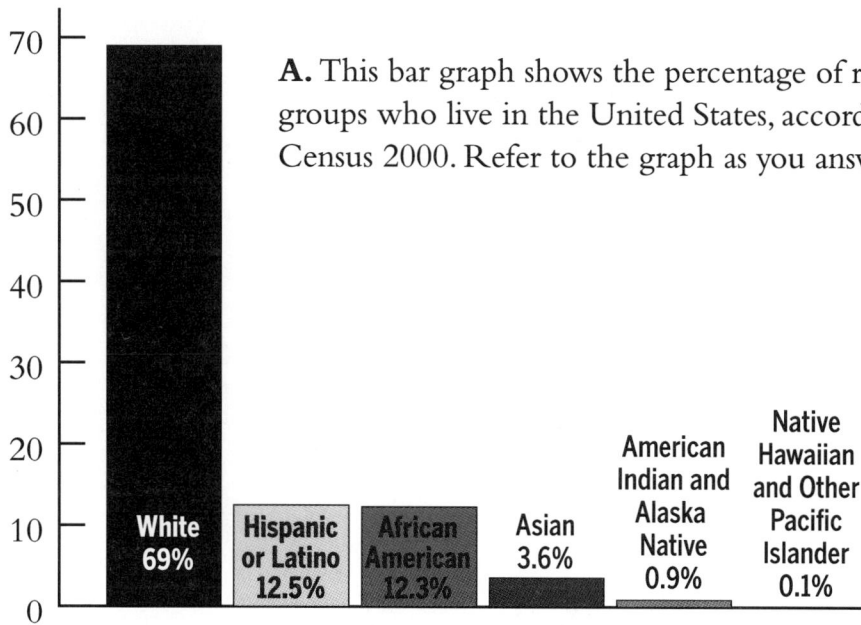

A. This bar graph shows the percentage of racial and ethnic groups who live in the United States, according to the U.S. Census 2000. Refer to the graph as you answer the questions.

```
70 |  ██
   |  ██
60 |  ██
   |  ██
50 |  ██
   |  ██
40 |  ██
   |  ██
30 |  ██
   |  ██                                    American    Native
20 |  ██                                    Indian and  Hawaiian
   |  ██                                    Alaska      and Other
   |  ██                                    Native      Pacific
10 |  ██   ████   ████   Asian              0.9%        Islander
   |  White Hispanic African  3.6%                      0.1%
   |  69%  or Latino American
   |       12.5%  12.3%
 0 |_____
```

1. Which bar on the graph is the longest? _____

   What does this tell you? _____

2. Which two ethnic groups are closest in size? _____

   How do you know? _____

3. What percentage of the population is either Native American, Alaska Native,

   Native Hawaiian, and Other Pacific Islander? _____

4. Which ethnic group makes up 3.6% of the population? _____

B. On a separate sheet of paper, create another bar graph that shows the areas from which Hispanic Americans come, according to the U.S. Census 2000. Your graph should show the following percentages:

Mexico: 66%

Central and South America: 14%

Puerto Rico: 14%

Cuba: 4%

Name_____

Census Takers

Refer to the book to find answers to the questions below. Circle the
letter of the correct answer. Then write the circled letters on the lines at
the bottom of the page to discover which language, other than English, is most
often spoken in homes across the United States

1. In which place are people most likely to *not* own cars?

r. Texas   s. Washington, D.C.

t. New York   u. Alaska

2. Which pet is the most popular in the United States?

m. cat   n. fish

o. rabbit   p. dog

3. How many elementary, middle, and high schools are in the United States?

a. 110,000   b. 11,000

c. 111,000   d. 1,100,000

4. How many people in the United States have computers?

m. 3 out of 100   n. 35 out of 100

o. 30 out of 100   p. none

5. To which state do most immigrants move?

g. Florida   h. Texas

i. California   j. New York

6. Which is the fastest-growing state?

p. New Jersey   q. California

r. Colorado   s. Nevada

7. How many people live in the United States according to the U. S. Census 2000?

h. 281.4 million people   i. 28 million people

j. 284 million people   k. 2.8 million people

Which language, other than English, is most often spoken in U.S. homes?

____   ____   ____   ____   ____   ____   ____

TIME FOR KIDS READERS

A Day in the Life of Washington, D.C.

BACKGROUND

Summary

When most people think of Washington, D.C., they imagine the White House, the Capitol building, and the Pentagon—and within those buildings, the inner workings of the U.S. government. However, there's more to Washington, D.C., than government. From museums and art galleries to parks and zoos, from exotic restaurants to close-knit neighborhoods, Washington, D.C., has a rich variety of offerings for residents and visitors alike.

READING TIPS

Building Background

■ What do you picture when you think of Washington, D.C.? Who lives and works there? What makes Washington, D.C., similar to and different from other cities in the United States?

■ Has anyone in the class ever visited Washington, D.C.? If so, invite them to share their impressions with the class. What did they see and do while they were there?

Reading For Details

■ How has the newspaper *The Washington Post* changed over the past 100 years? (It is now bigger, costs more money, and has more people working for it.)

■ Why is the Metrorail important? (Use of the Metrorail by commuters reduces the amount of traffic in the city.)

■ What is the oldest house in Washington, D.C., and in what neighborhood is it located? (the "Old Stone House" in Georgetown)

■ How has the purpose of the C & O Canal changed over the years? (The canal was once used to transport goods. Today bikers and hikers use it for recreation.)

■ If you wanted to see the Wright Flyer, where would you go? (the National Air and Space Museum)

■ In which building do the senators work? (at the Capitol building on Capitol Hill)

■ What important event happened on the Mall on the steps of the Lincoln Memorial? (Dr. Martin Luther King, Jr., gave an important speech there in 1963.)

■ Which D.C. neighborhood has a special festival to celebrate the neighborhood's cultural diversity? (Adams-Morgan has such a festival, called Adams-Morgan Day.)

Critical Thinking

■ How is Washington, D.C., different from other U.S. cities? Why is Washington, D.C., important to the rest of the United States? (Possible responses: It is our nation's capital; the federal government is

FAST FACTS

■ Washington, D.C., is not part of any state, but it is surrounded by two states: Maryland on the north, east, and southeast and Virginia on the southwest.

■ Washington, D.C., is named after two people: George Washington and Christopher Columbus (District of Columbia).

■ In 1800 the federal government was moved to Washington, D.C.

■ About a third of the people who work in Washington, D.C., have jobs with the federal government.

■ African Americans make up 60 percent of the population of Washington, D.C.

■ Although the population of Washington, D.C., has decreased since 1980, the populations of the surrounding suburbs in Virginia and Maryland have increased.

located there; the President and many other important government officials live and work there; the city contains many museums and monuments that reflect the history and culture of the United States.)

Vocabulary

architect: someone who designs buildings

canal: a channel that is dug across land to connect bodies of water so that ships can travel between them

diversity: variety

endangered species: a type of plant or animal that is in danger of becoming extinct

gallery: a place where paintings, sculpture, photographs, and other works of art are exhibited and sometimes sold

landmark: an object in a landscape that can be seen from far away

memorial: something that helps people continue to remember a person or an event

monument: a statue or building erected to remind people of a person or an event

EXTENSION ACTIVITIES

LOOKING AT IMAGES

Curriculum Area: Social Studies
Skills: Observation, Critical Thinking

Direct students' attention to the image on the cover of the book. Why do you think the designer chose this image? What does this image say about Washington, D.C.?

ALL AROUND THE TOWN

Curriculum Areas: Social Studies, Language Arts
Skills: Reading for Details, Note Taking, Categorizing
     Information, Descriptive Writing, Oral Communication

Distribute copies of page 67. Have students work in pairs to fill out the chart, noting what is important or interesting about each of the areas listed. Then ask students to imagine that they are tour guides whose job is to lead groups of tourists on walks through one of the areas listed. Have each pair select an area to research more fully, using print and Internet resources. Then ask them to write a short speech describing the area and pointing out special things

to do and see there. Have one partner from each pair present the speech to the rest of the class.

A CITY OF MONUMENTS

Curriculum Areas: Social Studies, Art
Skills: Interpreting Historical Events, Visual Design

Washington, D.C., is a city of monuments. Talk with students about the purpose of a monument—to help people remember an important person or event from the past. Then ask students to imagine that the city of Washington has just commissioned them to design a new monument to commemorate a person or event of their own choosing. Who or what would they choose and why? Have students draw sketches of their monuments and, if possible, create three-dimensional replicas.

ANSWER KEY

COPYING MASTERS

Page 67 Students should include at least two specific details about each topic.

Page 68 **1.** gallery, **2.** Metro, **3.** dome, **4.** Smithsonian, **5.** C & O Canal, **6.** Shaw, **7.** Mall, **8.** Georgetown; **Final Answer:** Adams-Morgan

READER

Think and Respond **1.** Without the Metrorail, the city's streets and bridges would be clogged with traffic. **2.** Possible responses: visiting the Smithsonian Institution, the National Zoo, the Capitol, the White House, or national monuments; listening to music in Georgetown; **3.** It is named after Capitoline Hill, one of the seven hills of ancient Rome. **4.** Students should consider similarities and differences between the daily life of their community and the lives of residents of Washington, D.C.

Do Research Students' presentations should include at least three significant details about the monument, building, or neighborhood they select.

Name_____

All Around the Town

The chart below lists several different places in Washington, D.C. Review the book and take notes about each place. Write your notes on the lines provided next to each topic.

The National Zoo _____

_____

_____

_____

Georgetown _____

_____

_____

_____

The Mall/Downtown _____

_____

_____

_____

The Shaw District _____

_____

_____

_____

The Adams-Morgan District _____

_____

_____

_____

Festival Day

Answer the questions below. Then write the numbered letters on the lines at the bottom of the page to reveal the name of a neighborhood in Washington, D.C.

1. What type of building houses works of art?

___ ___ ___ ___ ___ ___ ___
 9

2. What is the shortened name for the Washington, D.C., subway system?

___ ___ ___ ___ ___
 6

3. Which part of the Capitol building weighs 9 million pounds?

___ ___ ___ ___
 2

4. What is the name of the museum complex of Washington, D.C.?

___ ___ ___ ___ ___ ___ ___ ___ ___ ___
 5   11   10

5. Which waterway goes through the neighborhood of Georgetown?

___ & ___   ___ ___ ___ ___ ___
                              1

6. In which neighborhood is the new Washington Convention Center being built?

the ___ ___ ___ ___ District
                3

7. Where would you find the Lincoln Memorial?

the ___ ___ ___ ___
         4

8. In which neighborhood would you find the oldest house in Washington, D.C.?

___ ___ ___ ___ ___ ___ ___ ___ ___
         8   7

This Washington, D.C., neighborhood holds an annual cultural festival.

___ ___ ___ ___ ___ - ___ ___ ___ ___ ___ ___
 1   2   3   4   5   6   7   8   9   10   11

                                       A DAY IN THE LIFE OF WASHINGTON, D.C.

TIME FOR KIDS READERS

Becoming a Citizen

BACKGROUND

Summary

United States citizenship is something that most Americans take for granted, but that many immigrants hope to achieve someday. People born in the United States are automatically U.S. citizens. Immigrants who wish to become U.S. citizens can do so by following a procedure prescribed by the U.S. government.

READING TIPS

Building Background

■ What are some of the reasons that people decide to leave their home countries in order to immigrate to the United States? (Possible responses: political freedom, economic opportunity, education)

FAST FACTS

■ According to the U.S. Census 2000, 13 million people immigrated to the United States from other countries between 1990 and 2000.

■ The 28.4 million immigrants living in the United States make up approximately 10 percent of the nation's population.

■ An immigrant can become a citizen by going through a process called naturalization.

■ An immigrant can apply for citizenship once he or she has lived in the United States for five years.

■ The Immigration and Naturalization Act became law in 1952. The law sets forth guidelines for how to become a citizen.

■ The government body that oversees immigration is called the Immigration and Naturalization Service, or INS.

■ What is a citizen? (a member of a particular country who has the right to live there and to enjoy certain privileges, such as voting)

Reading for Details

■ How was Chun' Sook able to become a citizen, even though she was born in South Korea? (Chun' Sook and her family applied for citizenship and went through the naturalization process.)
■ What is the difference between a naturalized citizen and citizens? (Most citizens have citizenship upon birth. A naturalized citizen is a person who has become a citizen at some later point in life.)
■ What does the United States offer that some other countries do not? (the right to vote; freedom of speech; freedom of religion; good education; employment opportunities)
■ What do immigrants need to know in order to pass the citizenship test? (They must be able to speak English, and they must know basic facts about United States history and government.)
■ What are some things expected of new citizens? (New citizens are expected to vote, to serve on juries, and possibly to serve in the armed forces if the country goes to war.)

Critical Thinking

■ What do you think is the most challenging part of the naturalization process for most immigrants? (Possible responses: giving up citizenship of one's native country; taking the citizenship test; reciting the Oath of Allegiance at the swearing-in ceremony) Why?
■ Do you think most immigrants want to become U.S. citizens? Why or why not?

Activity

■ **Taking the Oath:** Distribute copies of page 71. Explain that these are the words immigrants say as they are sworn in as the final step in the process of becoming citizens of the United States. As a class, go through the words of the oath section by section, stopping to discuss what each section means. Then have students write paraphrased versions of the oath. Invite them to recite these reworded oaths to the rest of the class. Ask students how they think potential citizens feel as they recite the oath at their swearing-in ceremonies. (Possible responses: nervous, excited, hopeful, proud)

Vocabulary

allegiance: loyal support for someone or something

apply: to ask for something in writing

armed forces: all of the branches of a country's military

citizen: a member of a particular country who has the right to live there

citizenship: the state of or the rights, privileges, and duties that come with being a citizen of a certain country

democracy: a government in which citizens choose their leaders in free elections

immigrant: a person who comes from one country to live permanently in another country

immigrate: to move from one country to another to live there permanently

naturalize: to give citizenship to someone who was born in another country

oath: a serious, formal promise

public office: a position working for the government of a town, city, or country

swear in: to admit as a member, using the administration of a serious, formal promise

EXTENSION ACTIVITIES

LOOKING AT PHOTOGRAPHS

Curriculum Area: Social Studies
Skills: Observation, Critical Thinking

Direct students' attention to the photographs on pages 11–15 of the book, which show the swearing-in of new citizens—the last step of the naturalization process. Ask: How do these people reflect the larger population of the United States? (Possible response: The varying ages and cultural backgrounds of the people pictured reflect the growing diversity of the U.S. population.)

BECOMING A CITIZEN: A HOW-TO GUIDE

Curriculum Area: Social Studies
Skills: Research, Note Taking, Organizing,
    Visual Presentation, Group Work

Ask students to imagine that they have been hired to teach a class that will educate immigrants who wish to apply for citizenship in the United States. Have students work in groups to do research about the naturalization process, using print and Internet resources as well as the book. Each group will prepare a set of instructional posters that could be used in a citizenship class. Topics should include Who May Become a Citizen?; Steps to Becoming a Citizen; the Citizenship Test; and the Swearing-In Ceremony.

ANSWER KEY

COPYING MASTERS

Page 71 Possible response: I promise that I will be loyal only to the United States; that I will follow the rules of the United States and help protect the country against its enemies; that I will serve in the U.S. armed forces or help the United States in other important ways whenever necessary; and that I am making this promise because I truly want to.

Page 72 Students' word choices should be grammatically and semantically appropriate.

READER

Think and Respond 1. Since 1820, more than 40 million people have immigrated to the United States. **2.** Possible responses: religious freedom, economic opportunity, access to education, to flee danger; **3.** One must be at least 18 years old, be of good moral character, have been a lawful resident for at least five years, and be willing to swear loyalty to the United States. **4.** Possible responses: religious freedom, freedom of speech, voting rights

Write an Essay Students should cite specific contributions by people of various cultural backgrounds to the wider culture of the United States.

Taking the Oath

In order to become U.S. citizens, applicants must recite the Oath of Allegiance at the final swearing-in ceremony. Read the words of the oath below and discuss them with your classmates. Beneath each section, try to explain in your own words what that section means.

I hereby declare, on oath, that I absolutely and entirely renounce and abjure all allegiance and fidelity to any foreign prince, potentate, state, or sovereignty of whom or which I have heretofore been a subject or citizen;

_____

_____

_____

that I will support and defend the Constitution and laws of the United States of America against all enemies, foreign and domestic; that I will bear true faith and allegiance to the same;

_____

_____

_____

that I will bear arms on behalf of the United States when required by the law; that I will perform noncombatant service in the Armed Forces of the United States when required by the law; that I will perform work of national importance under civilian direction when required by the law;

_____

_____

_____

and that I take this obligation freely without any mental reservation or purpose of evasion; so help me God.

_____

_____

_____

Glad to Be Here!

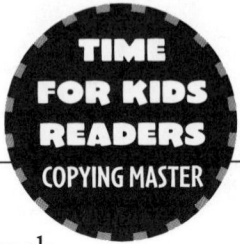

TIME FOR KIDS READERS
COPYING MASTER

The letter below could have been written by someone who recently became a United States citizen. Fill in the missing words to complete each sentence. The words below each line tell you the type of word you need.

Dear _____ ,
             (name)

    Today was a(n) _____ day! Today I became a citizen of the
                       (adjective)

_____ . It was a very _____ moment.
    (name of country)   *(adjective—feeling)*

About _____ people were in the courthouse. Everyone was
       (number)

_____ .
    (adjective—feeling)

    I spoke to a woman from _____ .
                              (country)

She moved to the U.S. _____ years ago. She moved here because
                (number)

_____

_____ .
    (reason for moving to the U.S.)

We expressed our _____ and _____ for the future.
             (noun)   *(noun)*

    I felt very _____ when I said the Oath of Allegiance.
           (adjective—feeling)

After the ceremony, many people _____ and _____ .
                 (verb)   *(verb)*

Do you know what I did? I _____ ! I will never forget this day.
               (verb)

It was the most _____ day of my life.
                (adjective)

        Your friend—and new U.S. citizen,

        _____
             (name)

© Harcourt

BECOMING A CITIZEN